Engstrom's Travel Experience Guides

A guide to a travel experience

Kenya Safari

By Barbie Engstrom

Foreword by Ron Smith

Illustrated with 175 photographs
8 in full color

Black and white photographs by the author

Color photographs by Fred Engstrom

An Original Kurios TO SEE AND ENJOY Book

KURIOS PRESS ■ Box 946 ■ Bryn Mawr, Pennsylvania

FOR THE ONE WHO CREATED THE ANIMALS
and for the one I love, my husband

Layout and design by the author

FIRST PRINTING
Library of Congress Card Number 78-16791
ISBN 0-916588-04-1
Printed in the United States of America

Grateful acknowledgement is given to Jane Levis Carter for permission to reprint her poem, *East Africa.* And portions of this book originally appeared in the travel section of the *Philadelphia Inquirer.*

Other To See and Enjoy books by Barbie Engstrom: PARIS TO SEE AND ENJOY
FAITH TO SEE

Engstrom's Travel Experience Guides in preparation: Egypt: Nile by Riverboat
Others planned: China!
India, Nepal and Bhutan: An Incomparable Trio

Note: the publisher has tried to insure the accuracy of the information in this book, but if you find any errors, please let us know. Also, names and portions of this book have been altered to protect the privacy of the trip members.

Library of Congress Cataloging in Publication Data
Engstrom, Barbie, 1937—
Kenya Safari.

(Engstrom's Travel Experience Guides)
"An original Kurios to see and enjoy book."
Bibliography: p. 138
Includes index.
I. Kenya—Description and travel. 2. Engstrom, Barbie, 1937-
I. Smith, Ron. II. Title. III. Title:Africa. IV. Series.
DT433.52.E34 916.76'2'044 78-16791
ISBN 0-916588-04-1

Contents

Description of Color Folio:

Page:	
129	Lion in Masai Mara Game Reserve, shot on an early morning run.
130	Lake Baringo, shot with yellow and star filters.
131	Njemp tribesmen, shot at Lake Baringo.
132-133	Sunset in Masai Mara Game Reserve.
134	Reticulated giraffe in Meru National Park; afternoon shot.
135	Cheetah, about two-years-old, in Masai Mara Game Reserve; noon shot.
136	Sunset in Masai Mara Game Reserve.

Publisher's Note:

If you want to order additional copies of this book, photocopy the handy coupon below and we'll be happy to send them to you. Or if you want to send them as gifts, we'll be delighted to enclose a gift card.

______ copies of *Kenya Safari.*
Name ______________________________
Address______________________________
City ______________State______________Zip______________
If a gift, sign card as follows: ______________________________
____
Ship now ______________Ship to arrive ______________

Postage chart for prepaid orders
(includes postage and handling)
Orders below $9.00 add—$.75
Orders from 9.01-17.00 add 1.25
Orders from 17.01-26.00 add 1.65
Orders over 26.01 add 2.25

______ subtotal.
______ Pa. residents add 6% state tax
______ postage and handling (see above chart)
______ total. Check/money order enclosed. No cash or C.O.D.'s please.
Mail to: Kurios Press, Box 946, Bryn Mawr, PA 19010
(please allow 2-4 weeks for delivery)

Foreword by Ron Smith

There is a song in the Swahili language that says, "God's handiwork is beautiful in Kenya."

Few travelers to this fascinating country would disagree. For those who look upon it, Kenya's awesome beauty has been astounding visitors for a long time. A century ago, two missionaries exploring its interior told stories about Mt. Kilimanjaro and Mt. Kenya. But they were scoffed at by the Royal Geographic Society. In deed, how could anyone believe that snow-capped mountains rose up along the equator?

Today, when people are increasingly sophisticated about travel, Kenya continues to surprise and astound with its wonders. It is Kenya, perhaps more than any African nation, which best reflects all the wonders of that vast and changing continent. Kenya has rain forests and barren plains, fertile farmlands and burning deserts, modern cities and backward villages, great animal preserves and beaches where tourists play.

I know of few travel writers who can look at the beauty of Kenya and appreciate it more than Barbie Engstrom. Rigorous research and painstaking attention to detail are the hallmarks of good travel writing. Barbie knows how to research. More importantly, she knows how to write; not just about places, but about people. Her work is personal as well as encyclopedic.

—Ron Smith, Travel Editor
Philadelphia Inquirer

Introduction

I discovered that I had to respond to a myriad of misconceptions when I went on an African safari. To many, "going on safari" conjures up visions of a train of porters following the wealthy hunter as he stalks wild animals. In fact, I was asked: "You didn't go to *kill,* did you?" Answer: No, but I shot a lot of pictures. The Kenya government has banned all big-game hunting, so all safaris are photographic.

Or, a safari means hardship. Some other questions were: "Was there anything to eat?" Answer: Some of the lodges were luxurious. "Wasn't it terribly hot in the desert?" Answer: The country is gorgeous; it's got cool mountains, rich farmland planted with everything from coffee to tomatoes and grassy plains that look like uncut golf fairways, as well as arid desert plateaus. "Weren't you afraid they would put you in a pot and boil you, like I saw on a TV show?" Answer: the people in many areas, especially around Nairobi, are educated—so much so that they are beginning to have a problem similar to ours in America—too many people wanting white-collar jobs.

Few people know that in Swahili, "safari" means just this: Any kind of journey (even a trip from New York City to Long Island) would qualify as a safari in a literal sense.

So, why go on a safari—especially to Kenya?

Kenya has always been the original safari country. Game is abundant and plentiful, the weather is straight out of the Caribbean, and nowhere else in the world can the traveler land at a busy international airport, clear customs, then four miles from town see herds of big game in the 44-square-mile Nairobi National Park.

Hunters and travelers from Teddy Roosevelt to Hemingway knew what they were doing when they crossed this Texas-sized country many years ago. And even today the safari picture hasn't changed in Kenya. It is a model among African nations in political stability and racial harmony compared with other African nations like Uganda whose problems, I might add, haven't rubbed off on the pro-West, tourist-loving Kenyans.

But you may be wondering what made us want to go? Answer: The desire for a quality vacation away from crowded museums and damp cathedrals; and interest in black culture; a love of the Lord's natural beauty and of animals, whose life I've always wanted to observe first-hand, and, as a photographer, the opportunity to bring back stupendous pictures.

But I must admit my husband, Fred, wasn't as enthusiastic as I. He pointed out the many reasons why a trip like this could be postponed. There were lots of other places he'd like to visit before Africa. And too, Africa wasn't going to disappear; it still would be there next year and the year after that. Also, what about the political situation? Laughingly, he reminded me of my mother's concern whenever we travel to parts of the globe which have the slightest turmoil. Then too, what were our chances of getting on a good tour? Our previous tour experiences had ranged from rather good to devastatingly awful.

Still, I wasn't about to be dissuaded. It was a matter of a childhood ambition. There were the dreams of elephants, zebras, giraffes, lions and all matter of wild beast roaming free—not behind the bars of a zoo. And it went back farther than that—to my father. He loved all the animals on the six farms he once owned, especially the newborn calves, and he instilled that love in me. In fact, I'm a sucker for animals. I remember as a little girl I used all my savings to purchase a mongrel from the Sunday want ads. Naturally, Fred knew all this. But I felt he needed an added incentive. I asked him if he would give me the safari trip as a special fortieth birthday gift. He couldn't say no.

Once again I turned to my friend and travel agent, Shirlene Johnson, for advice. I explained that we wanted a trip which would give us a minimum of hassle—even take us by the hand—in order to free us up to totally enjoy the animals and the environment. She immediately said, "The trip I took. I'm sure you would be satisfied." She added, lowering her voice, "The best way to go is on a wing safari where you fly from place to place. It's a bit more expensive but worth it. I've taken one and I'll tell you that we arrived at every spot refreshed, ready to go out and see the animals—."

Interrupting, I said, "I get the picture. We'll take the wing safari."

How did our safari work out? Were we satisfied? Yes! Words could hardly describe our enthusiasm. An African spell had been cast over us. Fred was in seventh heaven from being outdoors everyday; no phones ringing or stressful hassle for over three weeks. He was the most rested from this trip that I've ever seen him. We both wanted to go back—as soon as possible.

Lastly, what's the purpose of this book? Someone once said that if you obtain one tip or learn one new thing from a book, it's worth the price you paid for it. And I agree. So it is my hope you will find at least one item or suggestion between these covers that is of interest to you.

And with that in mind, I hasten to say, this book is meant to be a *guide to a travel experience* —or what's it REALLY like to go. Perhaps you are planning a trip to East Africa and want to know what you'll see and do on it. Or maybe you have been on safari and would like to relive it through these pages.

Also, I want to add, what this book is *not* meant to be. It will not be comprehensive (although when all is said and done, no book with the constant changes in life should be billed as all inclusive) on all the lodges or game reserves in Kenya. It will not give you population figures, historical-cultural background or in-depth wildlife descriptions. These you will find in books specifically published for that use.

Yet, I'd be remiss if I didn't mention this book is filled with tips on photography, etc, and the *How To* section at the back provides information important to the traveler.

So, in essence, this book is different from most guides—it relates a personal experience similar to memoirs, there's over 175 photographs such as you'd find in a lovely photography book, and you're given a section of practical information to help you plan your trip. Perhaps you'd say this is three books in one. But more than this, it's my desire that this book be *enjoyed,* and that you *see* the beauty which is Africa.

1/Safari Starts In Nairobi

WHAT'S IT LIKE TO GO ON SAFARI? It's fantastic!

To begin with, we were caught up in the excitement of Nairobi's International Airport as hosts of travelers, some already wearing safari outfits, disengorge from the huge jets; airlines from about 27 countries fly here, so you know the airport has to be *busy!* Approximately 400,000 visitors come to Kenya annually with only 20% of this total coming from America. I wondered if the Europeans knew something we Americans didn't.

A tip: arrive a few days early, if you can; the excursion fare is available for this. Then you'll be able to use the time to get over the long flight(s) or to shop for a safari outfit, let's say, or for some of the "buys" Nairobi's famous for.

Then, we were surprised to find Nairobi a luxuriously cosmopolitan town—no lions or buffaloes roam the streets. As a city of half a million population, it's not unlike Phoenix, Arizona with spacious boulevards dotted with palms and riotous masses of Bougainvillea, gleaming highrise office buildings, and new modern hotels.

Since we arrived three days early, we were on our own, so we bargained for the 20-minute taxi ride (about $8) to the New Stanley Hotel.

Along the way, we asked the driver to point out the various sights: the 44-square mile Nairobi National Park, renowned for its lions, but which is fenced in on the highway side; lush golf courses, as Nairobi boasts one of the ten best in the world; the futuristically modern Kenyatta Conference Center complex which has a revolving restaurant on the top of its circular tower; the house of Parliament and City Hall.

"What's that unusual round building?" I asked intently, as we slowed down in the downtown area.

"Oh, that's—," the driver answered nonchalantly, "the Nairobi Hilton."

Feeling nonpulsed, I was silent until we arrived at the New Stanley, located on a busy corner just two blocks from the Hilton.

Our tour brochure stated this older, but lovely hotel, was a traditional gathering place for safaris. And it's true. There's safari everywhere —from the lifesize panda bears appealing for funds to save the world's wildlife and the mahogany board listing the animals sighted at Treetops last night (6 rhino, 16 elephant, 89 buffalo, 39 bushbuck, 106 warthog)—to the tour "outfitters" (there are over 275 of them in Nairobi alone) touting trips and the melee of khaki-clad travelers, all heavily hung with cameras and binoculars, struggling, as we were, to get to the front desk.

How can you resist these appealing faces?

The New Stanley Hotel—a traditional gathering spot for safaris.

(Later we learned many were in line cashing traveler's checks; this can be a time consuming process as you are given a foreign exchange form at the airport which must be filled out properly and stamped each time you exchange currency; restrictions on money are tight.)

Finally, we were in the elevator on the way up to the room. My husband, Fred, said, "Whew! Wouldn't have believed it even if someone had told me. Yet, the registration went smoothly. Those guys at the front desk know their stuff."

Smilingly, I nodded.

Soon we were unpacked and attempting to take a nap in the Caribbean-like 85° weather and a non-air-conditioned room. (Later we switched to one with air-conditioning, paying extra, but this was largely a matter of preference, or perhaps being too Americanized on our part. A tip: if you go to the Norfolk Hotel, ask for the air-conditioned new wing.)

Our stomachs were growling when we awoke, so we decided to go downstairs to the outdoor restaurant at the New Stanley, called the Thorn Tree. (For more tips on good spots to eat, see the *How To* section at the back of the book.)

It's quite famous. It is said that Ernest Hemingway ate and drank here. And it's busy too. In fact, at times it's like an United Nations coffee klatch, as visitors from around the world stop here, some to place messages behind the wire mesh on the bulletin board, which serves as a lonely hearts bureau as well as a classified section of a newspaper.

"Look at this one," Fred said with a twinkle in his blue eyes. "It reads . . . *Nice Girl from New York Desires Ride to Ethiopia.*"

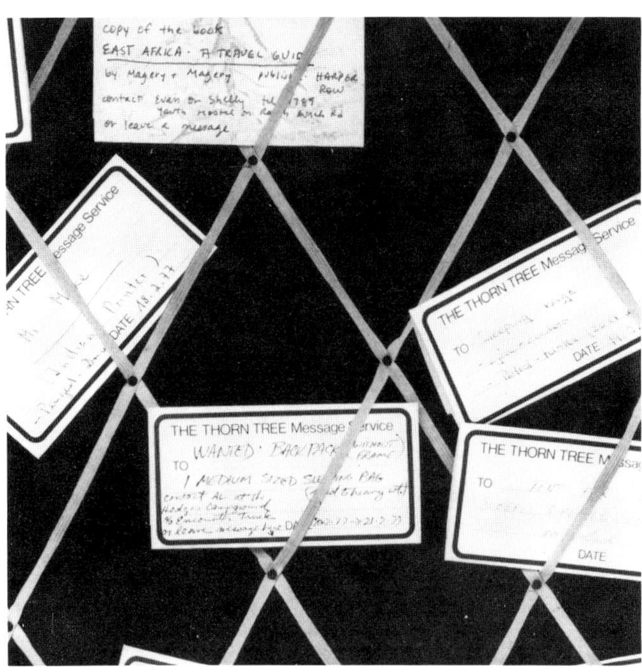

The Thorn Tree message service is used by travelers from near and far.

A meeting spot for travelers around the world—Thorn Tree restaurant.

THE NEXT DAY, we needed to purchase a safari outfit—or two (for a list of clothing needs and shop recommendations see the *How To* section at the back of the book). Even though it was Sunday, some of the shops (run by Kenyans of Indian descent) were open.

A dark-eyed proprietress dressed in a yellow silk sari informed us, "By all means come in, we'd be happy to serve you. What would you like—cotton or polyester—we have a wide selection to chose from."

And she did. I selected a khaki short-sleeve outfit whose slacks were miles too big for me. "Can you alter the waist for me?" I asked. "And what about the cuffs?"

"No problem, madam," the manageress said in a clipped British accent. "Our factory is open today till 2 P.M. We will have them for you. Don't worry."

Fred gave me a wink and motioned me over. He had decided upon two outfits, a white hunter's hat—wide-brimmed, trimmed in imitation leopard skin, dashing to say the least—and several Kenyan patches to sew on the sleeves.

A note on buying: bargain! That means for everything including clothing. The Indians are shrewd shopkeepers (and wealthy too, many drive Mercedes), and they love to bargain, while the African owners aren't so agreeable about "getting down the price."

As we were about to leave the shop a white-haired couple came in holding hands (Kenya attracts travelers of all ages). They were from South Carolina and had just come in from a safari. Why were they purchasing an outfit *after the fact?* Surprisingly, many people do. They explained to us that the red dust on the road safari had stained the man's trousers so badly that he needed a new pair. Also, they both wanted a good-looking outfit to wear back home.

A tip: if you are wondering how to get around the city—use the free map in *What's On* (found in your room or ask for one at the desk) with the Hilton as your landmark.

"BEFORE THE TOUR GROUP* arrives, let's see how much of Nairobi we can do on our own," I said to Fred. "The *Maridadi* magazine lists a slew of interesting places—like the Bomas of Kenya."

"Fine," Fred answered, "maybe we can hire a car and driver to take us around." (For information on how to do this, see the *What To Do in Nairobi* section in the back of the book. Also note: there are four attractions in Nairobi most want to see—the National Museum, the Snake Park, the Nairobi National Park and the Bomas of Kenya. It's possible to do all four in one day, although we spread it out over several afternoons.)

At the National Museum, we found Ahmed. "Did you ever see such a huge elephant?" Fred asked incredulously. "I sure wouldn't want to meet him face to face."

Ahmed is the world's largest elephant. He was protected by presidential decree so no one could poach him, until his death; but sorry to say, Ahmed's body wasn't discovered until it was too late—his skin was cracked and the best taxidermist in town, Zimmermans, said it wasn't possible to stuff him. So the next best thing was done—exact measurements were taken of the body and a perfect replica of Ahmed, complete with 200 pound tusks (each), now dominates the open courtyard adjacent to the museum.

Inside the museum, I said to Fred, "Did you know giraffes are *that* tall?"

He shook his head.

Towering over the main floor like a giant skyscraper was another stuffed animal, a 17-foot high giraffe.

Ahmed is Kenya's most famous elephant.

*(Editor's note: our tour was a wing safari which was very similar to the road or tent trips, the major difference being that we flew, thus saving time.)

Notice how small the people look compared to the giraffe.

The museum was mobbed with school children dressed in navy uniforms on field trips; they chattered away as we peered into diorama after diorama of the safari animals which proved to be a good introduction to their size, shape, and habitat.

Although the museum is an old structure, it houses a good East African bird section (again a good introduction to the unusual African birds) and on what could be called the mezzanine we found Joy Adamson of "Elsa the lioness" fame, has two major exhibits of watercolors, one of lovely East African flowers, and another of over 100 tribal portraits of ethnic African groups. (Most are surprised to find she was a fine artist long before her involvement with Elsa.)

Directly across from the museum (follow the signs) we paid a visit to the Snake Park which has some 200 varieties of snakes. I don't like these creatures but it was interesting—really—and the posted notices of "People throwing refuse into the crocodile pit will be forced to retrieve it" or "Trespassers will be eaten" were quite amusing.

Note: there's a new attraction in the museum complex, the recently completed (it was under construction when we were there) three-story International Louis Leakey Memorial In-

Look for the deadly snake inside this sign.

Traditional villages and . . .

bomas—huts—as well as . . .

stitute for African Prehistory. As you recall the late Louis Leakey built a strong case for Africa being the birthplace of the human race.

WILLIAM, OUR BURLY, TALKATIVE DRIVER told us that the Nairobi National Park and the Bomas of Kenya were located very close to each other, but were about a half hour's drive from the museum.

When I asked him what the Bomas were like, he answered, "It's a park where the government has set up villages from the various tribes like the Kikuyu or Luo to show the younger generation how our people did live. I come from a village like one in the park. I remember but some city people don't. Also, there's a main building where a group of dancers perform our native dances."

When we arrived at the Bomas he added, "We're early, so why don't you look around the villages first. There's a guided tour at 4 P.M. but I don't know if you want to wait for that."

As we walked in and out of the deserted villages, I said, "Why this is like an African Williamsburg."

"Yes, but without the candlestick makers and the various artisans," Fred added.

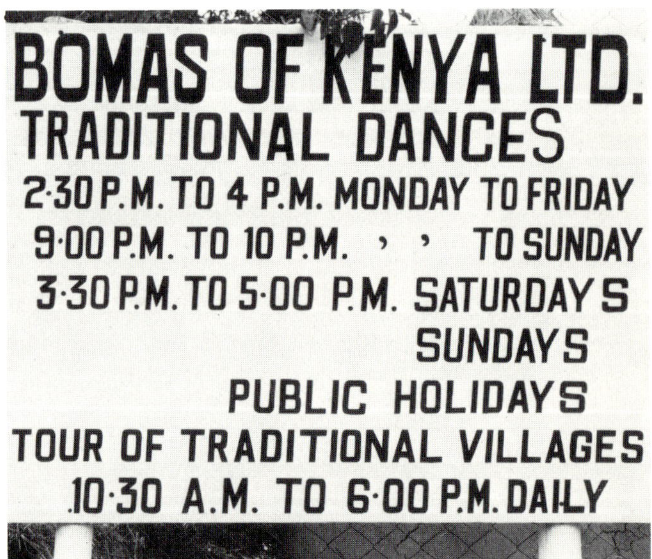

native dancing are all part of the Bomas of Kenya.

Too, the villages gave us the feel of tribal life. Later I learned the villages seemed so similar because all the tribes show a basic similarity of customs in that they were polygamous with the homestead consisting of a father and three wives. The first wife usually had an honored place in the society as she had the largest and most protected hut.

Yet, each homestead was constructed according to the tribe's traditions, such as the Kikuyu built only with split cedar while the Kisii smeared the walls of their huts with soil and cow dung; the thatching of the roofs differed from tribe to tribe too as did the act of entering the hut.

"What do you think?" I asked Fred as he bent down, almost knocking off his hat, to enter one of the bomas.

"No windows. But they're rather cozy inside." Then looking at his watch, he added, "It's almost time for the dancing to begin, so we better head back to the main building."

Along the way, we noticed some of the deserted villages were now populated with local women dressed in tribal costumes and incongruous green Bata tennis shoes. They were selling beads, carving and baskets. One lovely young thing would only allow me to take her picture if I purchased something. (For more on photographing the Africans, see the *How To* section.)

Isn't she lovely?

The dance troup is very professional.

When Willaim rejoined us in front of the beautifully striking vaulted structure which serves as the main building, I asked, "How long is the performance?"

"About an hour and a half. There's an intermission in the middle, but if you want to leave early that's fine."

We took a seat as close to the stage as possible and were greeted with a well-done program by a dance troup made up of members from Kenya's major tribes. The program listed 18 dances ranging from a Kikuyu circumcision ceremony to a joyful wedding dance.

Since our ears weren't accustomed to the unusual sounds coming from such instruments as the kayamba (flat rattles containing bean pods inside), we departed early. But the Bomas are well worth a visit just to experience a part of African tribal life that is dying and will only be seen in spots like this in the years to come.

A camera tip: the light isn't that good inside, so use fast film and sit close to the dancers; also bring a telephoto. A flash that has a range *past* 15 feet would help too. Usually I don't carry a tripod, but I could have used one here.

And the inside of the Bomas of Kenya is very dramatic.

THE NAIROBI NATIONAL PARK, almost around the corner from the Bomas, is regarded by some as one of the world's treasures of wildlife management; a friend who lived in Nairobi for several years said he rarely missed visiting this park on any given weekend.

And it's no wonder—the place teems with animals like zebra, giraffe, buffalo, wildebeast, warthog, baboon, ostrich, lion, leopard and cheetah—all with*in* the city limits. A low fence curving around the northern, western and eastern boundaries keeps the animals out of the residential areas and off the airport highway, but the animals roam freely into the vast Ngong National Reserve to the south. Note: this park was not stocked with game. This is "home" for thousands of animals; people intruded later.

At the park entrance, we stopped at the appealing wildlife orphanage, where young orphans found in the game reserves throughout the country are brought to grow up before being released back to the wild. As we walked the pathway from enclosure to enclosure we got a taste of what the animals looked like alive, not stuffed. And it was here we saw our first and only leopard of the trip.

Early morning and late afternoon are best for game-viewing, no matter what park you are in, so our 4 P.M. arrival was perfect. Armed with a newly purchased park map and guide, we entered the canopied forest, our eyes straining to detect any movement on our first game drive (this is the term used by the professionals indicating a visual search or hunt for animals).

"Velvet monkey," said William, meaning vervet monkey, pointing to a trembling tree with grey arms and legs scampering through it.

"Where?"

"There, at 1 o'clock." Fred answered activating his rarely used army jargon, which by the way, is used quite extensively to indicate locations of animals. Woe to the person like me, who finds this difficult.

Soon we reached a vantage point for a look at the Embakasi Plains below which was dotted with herds of impala, gazelle or eland, and the Nairobi skyline, gleaming in the distance like a technicolor mirage.

I almost had to pinch myself, it was so unreal.

As we stopped by a signpost pointing the way to the Hippo Pools (the roads are well-marked making it easy to tour this park), I asked, "Will we see lions today?"

The place to get a firsthand view of the animals is the Nairobi National Park animal orphanage.

Like a mirage, the Nairobi skyline glimmers in the distance.

William wrinkled his forehead and said, "Perhaps. I'll ask my friends if they've seen any." Then he shifted into low and we were off in a cloud of dust.

At that moment, I wasn't fully versed in the co-operation between the drivers as they tell one another of the location of the animals most tourists want to see. Soon we had a rendezvous with another driver who indicated in Swahili that a lion—*simba*—had been spotted near the Mombasa gate. Again we were off in a tan cloud.

So this is what a game drive is all about, I thought—it's a game of hide and seek with the animals.

(Note: throughout the book I will use plurals when talking about the animals which is Jane Goodall's method too, although there are some who call this a no-no. Naturally, I don't agree.)

Pulling off the road onto a barely visible track, William began to gesture wildly. "*Simba.* Lion," he said excitedly, indicating a spot of tawny color moving slowly in front of a VW van.

Sunset over the Embakasi Plains of the Nairobi National Park.

We converged on the van to find a very pregnant and hungry lioness. "We've been following her for two miles," said the van occupants, "and she's ready to give birth, so that's why she's so hungry."

As visions of a ravinous lioness snarling for food came to mind, I froze. So did Fred. Had we reached out of the open car window as she slowly passed our vehicle, we could have touched her. It was as if she was drunk. Her bloated stomach swung momentously almost causing her to fall several times. Not a camera clicked. We were spellbound.

In a way, the glorious sunset was anticlimactic as was the ancient black rhino we saw on the road leading back to the main gate. Our feelings were with her. Would she be all right?

Note: these animals live in the wild and take their chances for survival. That's why a zoo or an artificial game park can never be the same as the real thing.

Tiredness mixed with elation ended our day —certainly it was due to the sightseeing, but the visitor should be forewarned that Nairobi rests on a plateau which is more than a mile high, meaning the city is like Denver, so the atmosphere can contribute to any extra exhaustion.

ANOTHER CONCERN (besides the lioness) which was closer to home was packing the special suitcase that is mandatory on a wing safari due to the aircraft's limited luggage space. Prior to seeing it, I thought this could pose a problem—what if it is the size of an overnighter—I can never live out of *that* for almost two weeks. But my fears were unfounded. The brown, rather battered case, deposited next to our room the day before departure proved to be large and roomy; two additional carry-on bags allowed for the extras like film, guidebooks and other necessities. Our own suitcases, containing our city clothes, were to be left behind in the New Stanley's locked storage area; at the end of the trip we retrieved them, safe and sound, for a nominal fee.

A tip: good guides to have along are the *Animals of East Africa* by C.T. Astley Maberly (Hodder and Stoughton; paperback available in Nairobi shops; invaluable for information on the safari animals) and John G. Williams' *A Field Guide to the Birds of East and Central Africa* (Houghton Mifflin; hardcover, about $8.98; more expensive in Nairobi) if you are a birder, and even if you aren't as again it's invaluable.

Other books like Dinesen's *Out of Africa* are great to read before or after your visit but if space is limited, you'll find it is best to take the guides as the whole emphasis of the trip is on the animals and birds. Too, the lodge gift shops carry paperbacks, if you have time on your hands—which we didn't—to relax and read.

TONIGHT WE ARE TO MEET THE TOUR GROUP at a dinner and cocktail party. I was looking forward to this; usually the intimacy of touring together with a group produces a good friendship with at least one couple. Yet, I wondered what they would be like—Cassie Stinnett, the former editor of *Holiday* has said there is a world of difference between the tourist and the traveler. A traveler is one who loves adventure, while the tourist is—.

I'll have to wait and see.

After a thirty minute drive to a beautiful English tudor home in Karen, a lovely suburb of Nairobi (also the site of Dinesen's book) and an elegant dinner, we were briefed on what to do and not to do in the bush (see the *How To* section for these tips).

Too, our host told us many interesting facts about Kenya: coffee, not tourism, is the number one money maker in the economy; you'll rarely find chicken on the menu because they are all exported to the European market; there's an abundance of low cost food—for example, tomatoes cost 10 cents a pound; and dairy products are so rich that they have 2-3 times the butterfat content than Americans are used to.

Yet, he really caught my fancy with this story. He said, "When we first arrived about nine months ago, we didn't know that leopards would come across our back lawn to hunt. They come after dogs! We almost lost ours one night, so now we keep her indoors."

How exciting, I thought. That's Africa.

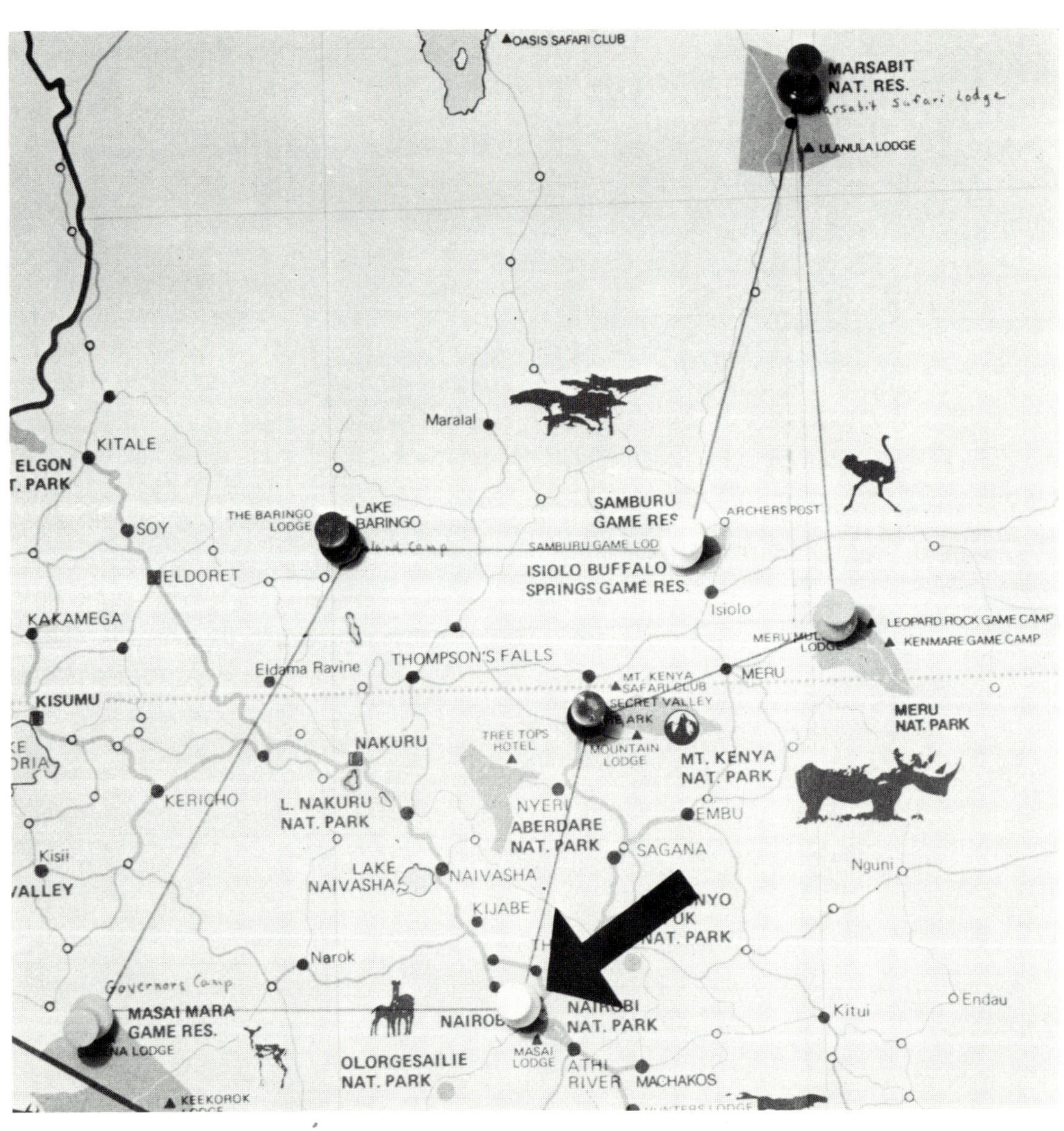

Map of our Kenya itinerary. Perhaps your safari will be different or changed. But the wonder that is safari never *changes.*

2/Off to the Ark

"WELL, TODAY'S THE BIG DAY!" Fred said with a big grin, his eyes twinkling.

"Right now, I've got cold feet," I answered. "While you were in the shower, I read an African magazine article entitled *Tea with a Vulture* at a spot we are to visit on the itinerary. The article said the place is so hot and desolate that even the crocodiles and vultures seek relief. Isn't that something? I wonder if this safari is going to be a hardship experience. And you know I'm not a camper— ever since those miserable days at girl scout camp with cold showers, awful wartime food made with powdered eggs and milk."

"Calm down," Fred interjected. "I enjoyed being in the field when I was in the army. It will be fine, just fine. Wait and see."

SINCE THE WING SAFARI was divided into two groups (A and B) of ten, our flight to Nyeri and the Aberdares by private Sunbird charter was set for 2 P.M.—just enough time to get a wash and set at the hotel's beauty salon, I thought (more on this later). I learned the afternoon flight was an economical use of the aircraft—the way wing safari costs are reduced—as Group B was sent one stop ahead on the itinerary, so they would always be waiting for our flight to transport them to their next destination. This arrangement proved advantageous to both groups; ours received a brief run-down on each spot from the embarking passengers, while Group B felt a certain one-up-manship until the last few days as they ended up at the Aberdares where Group A started, and some felt the Ark to be anti-climatic, while others said it was a fine place to "come off safari." To digress a moment and respond to those who might have a fear of flying in small planes, I can assure you that this is one of the most outstanding ways to see East Africa. The flights are low enough to enjoy the countryside, without subjecting your coccyx to the bouncing road trip (I've had back surgery so I'm especially careful). Sunbird Charters Ltd., is one of the best, if not *the* best in the air safari business. And the 3-engine Britten-Norman Trislander we used was a dream of a plane—originally outfitted with 18 seats, now it contains 10 which are extra-large with lots of leg-room and a full-view window for each passenger. It gives a smooth ride at 165 m.p.h. with a 700 mile range, and is almost like the commuter shuttle from Washington to Philadelphia. Our pilot, rather swashbuckling, Captain "Dickey" Bird was extremely experienced with over 20,000 flying hours. So relax.

"You mean it's possible to have your hair done in Africa?" asked an elderly friend who was planning an around-the-world trip.

"I didn't chance it in the bush. When it became unmanageable there, I put on my wig and plopped on Fred's khaki hat to keep off the dust. It worked out well. But to answer your question, sure there's beauty shops in most of the Nairobi hotels. Granted the New Stanley's wasn't exactly like the one I frequent at home in that it serviced both men and women. There was an Asian man next to me having his hair washed and blown dry while I was having mine set."

The woman's fears were quelled.

Freshly coiffed, I was ready for anything, especially the plane ride.

AT THE SMALL CRAFT AIRPORT located near town and on the edge of the Nairobi National Park, we met Ben, our tall, smiling African courier-guide. Earlier that day he had come off another tour, so we hadn't met him at the safari briefing last night. Now he was to accompany us everywhere seeing to the baggage, reservations, drivers, etc.—literally taking us by the hand so we could be completely free of hassle for almost two weeks in the bush. And above all, he was to play the invaluable role of spotting the East African birds and animals with such strange names as dik-dik or topi.

Married and a member of the Luo tribe, the second largest in Kenya located mainly on the eastern shores of Lake Victoria, bordering Uganda, and known for its writers and intellectuals, he was strikingly handsome; yet, his youthful features belied his forty years-of-age.

I asked him how he got into this business and he said, "It's good money and as the eldest son our traditions make me responsible for educating my brothers and sisters—two are in college now. My father can't, he's a minister, so—."

I liked his sincerity.

OFF TO WHERE MOST IMAGINE BIG-GAME VIEWING takes place—such spots as Treetops, where Princess Elizabeth learned she had become Queen of England in 1952, or the newer, more isolated Ark, both about a three-hour drive from Nairobi or 45 minutes by air, and located in the heavily forested Aberdare National Park which for the most part is 7,000 to 13,000 feet above sea level, and is overshadowed by 17,000 foot Mt. Kenya and the Aberdare Mountains, thus giving you the feel of a bit of Scotland in Africa.

Our flight to Nyeri, the closest town to the Ark, was over lush rolling countryside reminiscent of Gauguin with orange-red earth, and acid green banana trees.

Who said Africa was all desert?

Our itinerary listed two days here, one night at the Aberdare Country Club and the other at the Ark. Later I learned other safaris spend one night at the Ark or Treetops, then head north to Nanyuki and Bill Holden's Mt. Kenya Safari Club. Yet, I was pleased with our arrangements—the Aberdare Country Club boasts only five rooms, is noted for its gourmet candle-lit dinners set in a paneled English drawing room, has a

Gauguin would have been happy to paint this lovely rolling countryside.

The Aberdare Country Club is nestled in what's called the highlands of Africa. Notice the croquet mallets.

magnificent garden of jacaranda and flame trees replete with strutting peacock, and is country clubby in name only, as it's the transfer point of people and baggage for the Ark (the Outspan Hotel is similarly used for Treetops). Prior to observing the transfer operation, I wondered why it was necessary, but now I know that the Ark or Treetops, for that matter, are isolated water-holes and you can well imagine the chaos which would ensue if travelers just dropped in to stay the night—so all bookings are done in advance with the country club serving as the check-in point.

ARRIVED IN TIME FOR LATE LUNCH—a sumptuous spread of creamy chicken, fish in aspic, beef curry on fluffy rice, chutney, an assortment of vegetable salads, fruit, sweets and yummy Kenya cheeses.

A game drive was scheduled for 4-6 P.M. in the rarely explored, but oft visited, ravine-filled Aberdare National Park. Here, in an area of 228 square miles, hidden trout streams flow and waterfalls cascade down hundreds of feet of rock, but it's the thrill of the rollercoaster ride in the Land Rover which was memorable (in fact, this afternoon was one of the highlights of the trip).

After we entered the gates to the park, the driver held his finger to his lips and said, "Shhhh," in an attempt to aquaint us with safari etiquette—no talking, it scares the animals. This turns out to be a wonderful rule—imagine getting away from your job and having silence enforced for almost two weeks.

A limb cracked, swaying in the afternoon breeze. "Colobus," said the driver.

"Where?"

At a height of about three stories, the beautiful but rarely seen, except in forested areas, black and white colobus monkey swung from tree to tree, its long silky mantle flowing like a magician's cape in the breeze.

To see a troop of them, black faces ringed in white, leaping gracefully, almost non-monkey like in that they are silent by nature, is fascinating.

Around the corner munching like lazy cows chewing the cud were a group of cape buffalos—some weigh close to a ton. Tourists mistakenly call them "water" buffaloes. Some even say for their size they are surprisingly timid, but they look mean and when provoked they *are* mean. Their only natural enemy is the lion who prefers to pick out a calf or cow, when possible; cantankerous bulls often kill lions. When wounded, this animal is one of the most vindictive in attack and even in an unmolested setting like the park, we felt watched by them, instead of the other way around. One bull with horns almost three feet across snorted—would he charge; we decided to move on.

"Meru bushbuck at 11 o'clock," said the friendly driver. All heads turned left.

"What was that name again?" asked someone, usually the non-photographing member of the group appointed to write down the names of the animals. "I can't find it in this guidebook."

"Meru, meru bushbuck," reinterated the driver.

Ben winked. "He means *male* bushbuck."

Note: we had the best time with the drivers. They couldn't have been more accommodating, and their fractured english caused large amounts of good humor.

Running like a bat out of ____ was a giant forest hog, a shaggy black boar, weighing up to 300 pounds with tusks protruding below the eyes. He's strictly a forest animal and his ugly black bulk gives the impression of a small rhino or a buffalo.

Rhino gates guard the entrances of most national parks in Kenya.

Perched on top of your vehicle, you get a bird's eye view.

A cape buffalo gives you the "eye."

But the wild pig we liked the best because his tufted tail stands stiffly upwards like a riding crop when running, is the warthog. It's a devil to get a picture of him, however, he's so fast.

By now the light was beginning to fade and we couldn't get readings even with fast film. It was cool. I was looking forward to a hot bath and a fire in the fireplace.

Back at the club, a tour member asked us to fix a camera he had borrowed to take along on the trip.

A tip: know your equipment before leaving home. But don't let me deter you from purchasing or borrowing a camera equipped with a telephoto lens just for a trip of this type. Personally, I'd sooner take my chances, as there is usually someone in the group who is familiar with cameras to help you out in a pinch, than to come home with poor pictures.

During the cocktail hour as we sat around a roaring fire, luscious cashews which had been warmed in the oven were served. Yet, it was the dinner menu, written in Swahili and English, that was unbelievable, considering you were in the mountains in the middle of nowhere.

The giant forest hog is not the most beautiful animal in Africa.

Fresh Orange Cocktail
Machungwa Na Sukari

Cream of Peas (Soup)
Supu Mzito Wa Aina Moja Ya Mboga

Tournedos Arlesienne
Kipande Cha Sarara Ya Ngombe, Nyanya Na Mkate

Saute Potatoes
Viazi Vyembamba

Vegetables in Season
Mboga Ya Majira

Cream Caramel
Chakula Kitamu Na Sukari Uliyounguzwa

Cheese and Biscuits
Jibini Na Biskuti

THE NEXT MORNING—ARK DAY—twin-peaked 17,000 ft. Mt. Kenya showed its summit as the cloud cover disappeared for about 10 minutes. Like 19,000 ft. Kilimanjaro, located in Tanzania, it has a mystic all its own. (The Africans believed it to be the house of *Ngai*, God. Too, they called it Ke'Nyaa for the black and white cock ostrich. The early Europeans took this as a name symbolizing the land's harsh contrasts and named the area Kenya.)

It had rained last night, making the steep inclines and rough park roads impossible to negotiate, so the game drive was cancelled and we were going to the market in Nyeri instead. The shoppers in the group were delighted.

The native market was just that—for the natives. No rows of carved animals or tourist things to buy, only vegetables, pots and pans, cooking charcoal and other necessities of life for the land-tilling Kikuyus, the largest tribe of over 2 million in Kenya and reputed to have formed the basis for the Mau Mau strength in the early 1960's .

Still, one member of the group came away with a handsome hand-carved mahogany walking stick for a few dollars and I bought a few yards of colorful cloth.

Nyeri has quite a large British population as a visit to the local Episcopal Church will tell you. Adjacent to the church is Lord Baden Powell's grave, the founder of the Boy Scouts, who died in England but wished to be buried in Africa where he served in the military. Like so many Britons, attested to by the many hand-polished memorial pews to Sergeant-Major so-and-so, on his tour of duty he had lost his heart to the grace and beauty which is Africa.

A well-spent morning.

Glorious Mt. Kenya rises its head skyward.

TRANSFER TO THE ARK goes off like clockwork. After lunch, the tangle of luggage and passengers, departs *in toto,* at a specified time, for dinner, the night and the next day's breakfast with departure at 7 A.M.

Prior to leaving, the bird aviary, a good huff-and-puff walk below the club, was visited; it was the only spot where we were able to get close to the beautiful national bird of Kenya, the crowned crane.

A tip: allow enough time to photograph the birds here (we didn't); you'll get good shots without a lot of hassle. Africa has so many striking birds that if you're not a bird watcher, you will be one by the time you get home.

Like a caravan, the big tour bus followed by the Land Rovers, wound through the park to the Ark. Nobody spoke, although every once and a while someone would point at a spot where an elephant or buffalo head was sighted.

In the distance, like an isolated cabin deep in the primevil forest, appeared the Ark.

Noah would have been proud of this place. It boasts: snug nautical cabins with orange wool blankets standing out against the dark wood decor; a first-rate dining room; glass enclosed viewing lounges where drink in hand you can

The Ark, whose architecture is exactly like its name implies.

The crowned crane is easily recognizable by the straw-colored tuft on the top of its head.

watch the animals come to drink at the water-hole seeded with salt; and on the ground floor, an eye-level pillbox for photographers.

Yet, the Ark is more than its fine facilities—its a hushed drama which begins when you realize you have to cross a long drawbridge over a treacherously steep but beautiful gorge to get into the place.

Part of the drama too is Mr. Hardy, the "white" or professional hunter, whose instructions were: you won't be able to leave the Ark until the next morning as the drawbridge will be closed to prevent animals from entering; always remain quiet, the animals don't like noise; the 15,000 watt artificial light flooding the water-hole serves as a moon in the evening and will allow you to watch and photograph (more on this later) the animals; every cabin has a buzzer which will be sounded at anytime during the night when interesting animals appear—remember two buzzers mean elephant or rhino while three buzzers are for leopard or bongo.

The animals like actors arrive at the Ark while the people audience watch.

Mr. Hardy, garbed in typical professional hunter attire of gun, binoculars, etc.

Like a group of schoolkids on a fabulous field trip, we boarded the Ark.

Inside, long passageways led to the rooms—ours, on the second deck (the first deck has only 6 rooms, all with bath, which are reserved years in advance), were well-situated overlooking the left side of the swampy water-hole where from the screened-in window (porthole) we could observe the comings and goings of the animals. Community bath facilities prevailed (oh well, I thought, one night without a shower never hurt anyone).

For the first hour aboard, the place was abuzz as the almost 80 occupants of the Ark explored the open observation deck, the floor-to-ceiling glassed in lounges, the pill-box, and almost every nook and cranny of the ship.

Then almost everyone settled comfortably into the leather lounges, drink in hand, to wait for the animal show to begin. I expected elephants to arrive first but it was a herd of cape buffalo, far off in the distance who were sighted initially.

Slowly, ever so slowly, almost shyly, they came to front and center stage; someone counted 34. People excitedly pressed their faces against the glass; cameras clicked.

Hurriedly, we went out on the small open observation deck on the left side where they passed no more than five feet away. Backs caked with mud, they shook their massive heads, emitting grunts and groans, but nervously moving on. We could smell them and visa-versa.

Night was coming on with all the sounds of the marsh symphony.

We were tensely quiet.

Attempting to get good photographs, I spent a lot of time going up and down the stairways to the various observation areas (there are 3) and the ground floor pill-box. But the lighting on a rainy day made my efforts almost futile. Flash is not allowed—it scares the animals; and even the night photography guide for lodges which I had purchased at the club's gift shop (a good one, though small) was of no help.

A tip: under adverse conditions don't waste your film. You can try time exposures in the pill-box which I enjoyed visiting (only two are allowed in at a time) but don't expect much as the animals are constantly moving, so you get a blur. A tripod is not necessary either.

At dinner (delicious too, almost as good as last night's), the conversation turned to the elusive bongo, which sounded like a drum to me. At first I thought someone was pulling my leg. "What is it?" I asked.

"A striped deer, really an antelope," Ben said.

Who ever heard of a *striped* deer. Imagine bambi with stripes. Come to find out though, the bongo is a large eland-like antelope with spiral like horns tipped in ivory and whose dark brown body sports about thirteen snowy white vertical stripes; a zebra in reverse. It's very rare and found only at spots like the Ark.

The lovely dining room at the Ark.

Feeling unfamiliar with the animals and their names, someone laughingly said, "I wouldn't know a bongo, if I fell over one."

"Once you've seen one buffalo, you've seen them all," another chimed in.

"For me to recognize a bongo," said another, "it's going to have to carry a sign, I AM A BONGO."

Later, after dinner, while sitting around the fire, a large-spotted genet cat appeared on the observation deck and clawed at the door to get in. The genet whose total length from nose to tail tip is about three feet looks like a miniature leopard; noted for being bloodthirsty, it's a nocturnal creature, rarely seen by day. But this beauty was a pet of the white hunter's and all it wanted was a few tidbits.

Still, I felt a sense of timelessness pervading the long night. Noiselessly the animals departed and arrived. So did the passengers on the Ark, as they shuttled back and forth from area to area. It was as if we were entombed—perhaps on a space ship that was hurling us millions of light years beyond.

Then two buzzers sounded, doors slammed, and footsteps apppeared out of nowhere. Elephant.

"I have a feeling we're not going to get much sleep tonight," Fred said. "Should we go to bed with our clothes on?"

A woman passed wrapped in a sweater, noiselessly padding back to the room in bed slippers.

"Let's get into our p.j.'s," I answered. "If three buzzers sound for a bongo or a leopard, we can wrap ourselves in a blanket and go out."

The next morning, almost like a golf scorecard, the posted record of animals was:

buffalo	56	rhino	1
warthog	2	elephant	1
hyena	10	genet cat	1
bushbuck	30	African hare	1
giant forest hog	25	white-tailed mongoose	1

Still, neither a bongo nor a leopard was sighted. Perhaps you could call it two over par.

The striped bongo is the third animal to the right.

3 / Meru — Home of Elsa the Lioness

ARRIVAL IN MERU NATIONAL PARK at 9:05 A.M. made us feel like we were in the *real* Africa. Here was: miles and miles of rolling blond bush dotted with flat-topped acacia trees and doum palms; herds, not just one or two, but family groupings of elephants slowly lumbering past our eyes; a vast blue sky filled with fluffy clouds; and heat like a blast furnace making us shed any long-sleeve apparel.

This is the domain of Elsa the lioness of Joy Adamson's book *Born Free* (take some time to read or reread this book and also *Pippa's Challenge* about a cheetah who lived here too, so you can get to know this area). As I looked around, I recalled this park was chosen for Elsa's second and final release (she died here and is buried on the Ura River, a small gravestone marking the spot) because it's well-watered, three rivers flowing through the 700 square miles, and it's wild and quite unspoiled due to being off the beaten tourist track, located 180 miles, largely over unpaved roads, from Nairobi.

Our accommodations for two nights were at the Meru Mulika Lodge whose airstrip was only a short walk from the front door. It's a government operated facility, built in 1974, in the form of rondavel's with thatched roofs, which gave you the feel of living in an African *boma* or

There's a feel of Africa at the Meru Melika Lodge.

possibly a dude ranch under thatch.

Two things caught my eye: the portrait of the President of the Republic of Kenya; and the cool veranda where I imagined we could sit and watch the elephants browsing on the plains.

Others spotted the swimming pool. But David, the tall, handsome, ultra British manager, informed us that the filter was not working, so swimming was at your own risk; the normally blue pool was algae green.

Ben informed us of the daily schedule (which didn't vary that much during the remainder of the trip): lunch, 12:30 to 2 P.M., reserved at a long table for the group, including Ben; afternoon game drive, 3:30 to 6 P.M.; dinner, 7:30 to 9:00 P.M.

The next day, the same with a morning game drive, 8:30 to noon. The full day's game run with a luncheon barbecue along the river was cancelled, which was fine, considering the heat, we'd be the ones barbecued. Breakfast was at 7:30 A.M., and if anyone wanted 6:30 tea or coffee brought to the room, it had to be ordered the evening before (times have changed; usually this service, which everyone loves, was done automatically but now it must be ordered in advance).

"That doesn't leave much time for relaxing around the pool," someone said laughingly.

After last night's animal festivities at the Ark, many of us felt almost hung-over.

(Some members of the group told me later that they had brought along quite a few paperbacks to read in their spare time, but now due to the full schedule, they wished they had used the space for clothes, like a sundress or a skirt).

"AH-HA," I said to Fred, "there's enough time before lunch to do the hand laundry we've accumulated."

"I heard there's a laundry service," he answered. "It's not same day, but if we get it in today, it will be back tomorrow afternoon."

Little did I know then how laundry is handled in Kenya—all of Kenya, even suburban Nairobi. After it's washed, sometimes pounded by hand, it's spread on the ground, over bushes, hung from trees or anything to allow it to air dry. Electric clothes dryers don't seem to exist and at times, neither do clotheslines. Still, when all was said and done, most of the laundry (cost is nominal) came back beautifully done except one cotton tee-shirt which apparently received too much "tender loving care" now was permanently grey.

A tip: bring enough plastic hangers and even a clothesline to accommodate all your hand laundry. We purchased 50% cotton and polyester socks and underwear for Fred to take along as 100% cotton, when rain hits, such as it did in Mara, doesn't dry.

In spite of David's warning, the rest went swimming, causing those who put their faces in the polluted water to contact an eye infection; fortunately, one member of the group, a doctor, had brought along a small supply of medicines for such an emergency, so he held "clinic" before lunch.

A tip: be as careful about the water in the swimming pool as you are about the water you drink.

Another tip: bring along a small first-aid kit which contains a small plastic container of rubbing alcohol and a tube of calamine lotion. I got a case of chiggers from wearing sandals (wear socks at all times) and needed both.

PRIOR TO LUNCH, Fred took up residence on the cool veranda overlooking the vast African wilderness. "Take a look at those elephants," he said, handing me the binoculars. (A personal note: since I'm always looking through a camera lens, I don't own a pair of binoculars. But in Africa there will be times when you will not be taking pictures, and you'll just want to *look*—so borrow or buy your own pair to bring along.)

The spot to relax and watch the elephants go by—the cool veranda.

To some, elephants are "bad" animals, noted for being tempermental and unpredictable. Signs in some parks—ELEPHANT HAVE RIGHT OF WAY—tell the visitor to give them wide berth. But ever since reading the Douglas-Hamilton's book, *Among the Elephants* (this is a delight to read before, during or after the trip), they've held a certain fascination for me. Here's the largest animal in the world whose behavior in some aspects parallels that of man; they have been known to bury dead bodies under heaps of vegetation, and they've been observed carrying away the tusks and bones of their comrades, dropping them some distance beyond, as if in some necromantic rite. (Note: the tale of an elephant graveyard is just that—a fable.)

I especially like these things about them: they way they flap those massive ears like giant fans; the sounds of a herd drinking, ranging from a slurp to deep rumbles; their nerve-racking trumpeting when angry; the way their trunk rhythmically goes up and down searching the air; and their walking, plodding along at an estimated 4 m.p.h., which can be increased to 10

"Don't come too close," this elephant seems to say.

m.p.h. under stress.

David, the manager, talked at great length with Fred about the dwindling number of elephants due to poaching. And he also mentioned the destruction elephants in great numbers can wreak, such as that seen in Tsavo National Park (see Peter Beard's book, *The End of the Game*). I gather this park became a wasteland due to overpopulation and more than 20,000 animals perished due to starvation. (However, others have said things aren't as bad as depicted in this book.)

Note: you may wonder why I haven't gone into greater detail about conservation and other issues—well, I don't feel this is within the scope of this book.

THE LUNCHEON BUFFET was a feast fit for a king: warm curried beef, cold ham, chicken, roast beef, corn, lettuce, tomatoes, mounds of shredded carrots, baked beans, a wide variety of mousses, and Kenya cheddar cheese. But the steaming celery soup stopped us in our tracks; who would believe that hot soup on a 100° day

Elephants have the right of way in all African game parks.

would be cooling—but it is. Throughout the whole trip homemade potato, pea, asparagus—you name it, we had it—soup was served; it was delicious.

LATE AFTERNOON GAME RUNS proved to be my favorites. The light is warm for photography and the animals abound, searching for dinner. This afternoon's was the first of many in the dry heat, bouncing along on dusty tracks as waist-high thornbush grated the sides of the van like fingers drawn across a blackboard (cars, as you can well imagine, take a beating here).

Some imagine, since the vistas stretch for miles, that it's easy to spot the game—well, it isn't—the "bush" reduces visibility to a few yards. Your eyes strain to detect any movement.

The bush moves. The driver shuts off the ignition, allowing the van to coast to a halt. "Male waterbuck," Ben said, indicating a large shaggy coated, brownish antelope, weighing a couple of hundred pounds.

"Sure that isn't *meru* waterbuck," someone suggested.

Ben laughed. "No, it's a male, the females don't have horns. And it's the common ringed type. Take a look."

Sure enough a ring circled its rump, making the tail the center of a bull's eye. I smiled at the Creator's humor.

"The guidebook says they smell like turpentine," someone added.

"Never got close enough to know if that's true or not," Ben patiently answered.

Suddenly the male bushbuck bolted out of sight.

Again we took to the dusty road, searching, always searching.

The vast African bush stretches from horizon to horizon.

"LOOK, LOOK! A GIRAFFE in the middle of all those zebras," someone said excitedly.

"Get closer!"

"They are moving away!"

"Hurry."

"Stop. I want to get a picture."

"Shhh!"

"Ouch."

"What happened?" someone whispers.

"I banged my head again trying to get through the open hatch."

The intensity and excitement of any game drive is hard to put into words. Although everyone knows the safari etiquette of quietness, etc., it takes some time to learn the ropes of standing in the open hatch (only two can fit at any one time); identifying the animals and keeping a list; rotating seating in each van so everyone can get a chance to be by a window.

A tip: be flexible. With two vans and eleven people including Ben, plus the driver of each car, it's impossible for everyone to have a window seat *all* the time. Also, don't monopolize the hatch. Personally, I found it's not necessary to be in the open hatch to take good pictures—almost every shot in this book was taken from the front

Notice the bull's eye rump on this male waterbuck.

Safari is a visual search.

seat (with a 300 mm lens) where I sat next to the driver; naturally there had to be some readjustment on my part when the game was on the driver's side, still there was no problem, if he ducked out of the way.

Also, if two couples are traveling together, split up now and then in order to know the other members of the group. Note: even couples may have to split up to avoid overcrowding any one van. Too, the guide-spotter like Ben, can't be in two places at one time, meaning this person will have to be shared—one van in the morning, the other in the afternoon.

Additional camera tips: bring a few large plastic bags to cover the camera so your equipment won't get covered with dust. With the telephoto, set the aperture at f11 or 16 for good depth of field—then your pictures will turn out sharp; don't worry if your shutter speed is less than 250. A "sandbag" is *not* needed to steady the telephoto (I brought along a canvas bag filled with lentils which I didn't use once). Obtain a polarizing lens for color or your photos will be washed out by the light intensity; for black and white, I used a red filter almost all the time.

A last tip: for those who will not be taking pictures, a small notebook to list the animals will be a help to you and the group (many times we copied someone's animal or bird list in the quiet of our room).

DISAPPOINTED the towering giraffe and the zebra herd had moved away so quickly, we set out to find another grouping. Suddenly, out of the bush like giant moving cranes three giraffes ambled into the middle of the roadway and froze.

"Oh—h—h!" we almost said in unison.

"Aren't they something!"

These creatures, the tallest of all mammals,

The way to tell a reticulated giraffe is by the network of white lines on the body.

were of the reticulated subspecies, marked by a network of narrow white lines, giving them the appearance of a giant jigsaw puzzle. (This species is not as common as the spotted Masai giraffe.)

Without the slightest show of fear, they stared at us out of liquid brown eyes under long eyelashes. Many find this animal to be their favorite; Isak Dinesen in *Out of Africa* called them "giant flowers." And they do have a gentle radiance about them.

I find them to be marvelously made: the lungs, being oversized, have extra air-pumping capacity to compensate for the dead air volume in the long neck, otherwise the animal would breathe the same used air over and over; and a wonderful network of blood vessels in the head keeps the blood pressure constant in the brain so the giraffe does not have a fatal hemorrhage when it bends down to take a drink.

Click, click, went the cameras. Silently they moved across our path, giant melancholy eyes peering down on us. Someone let out a long, loving sigh. "I'll drink to that!" was the response.

The black and white buffalo weaverbird is a noisy character.

MORNING IS THE BEST TIME FOR THE AFRICAN BIRDS, which come in a rainbow of colors. In the acacia trees outside the room, members of the largest bird family in Africa resided—the white-headed buffalo weaverbird. Seemingly by the hundreds, this noisy finch-like bird was perched beside a unique globe-shaped structure of a nest, made of straw, 6-8 inches in diameter, hanging like jack-o-lanterns hung for some festivity from the woodland trees.

For protection, the nests are woven upside down. I wondered why the eggs or chicks didn't tumble out the bottom hole.

THE MORNING GAME DRIVE yielded other birds whose plummage was as outrageously color-keyed as their names: European roller with brilliant blue wings, baby blue body and light chestnut back; or white-throated bee-eater with pale green below the crown merging to beautiful blue on the long tail feathers and cinnamon wings.

Look at these unusual nests dotting this tree.

And I'm not a birder either; yet, you can't help but be excited about the African birds.

Note: more often than not, you will discover that someone in your group is an ornithologist or is maintaining a life list. These individuals are invaluable; they know how to identify what you are seeing.

Camera tips on birds: a 500 or 600 mm telephoto lens is a must. An ornithologist we met had a 1000 mm lens attached to a small tripod.

Like the birds, the animals have strange names and unusual markings too. We had been out about two hours, fording the river, lined with doum palms, the only Y-branched species of palm in the world, several times when we chanced upon a small herd of antelope with black and white faces.

"Oryx," Ben whispered, "oryx *beisa* but they won't stay around long enough to have their picture taken."

Looking like late revelers for a masked ball, they left immediately just as Ben said.

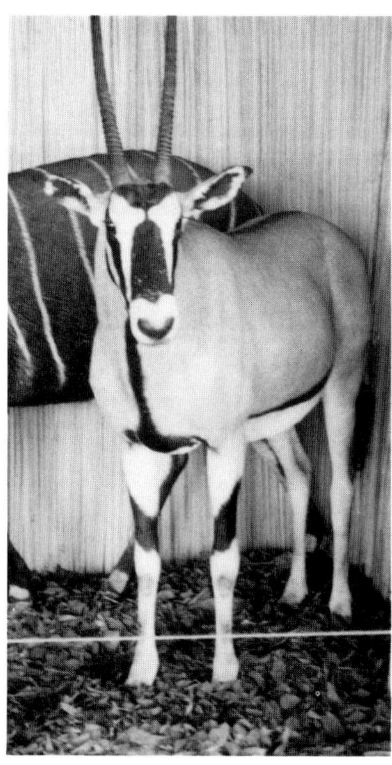

The Nairobi Inter-Continental has a stuffed oryx in its lobby.

This shy and beautifully marked animal is wary by nature and you have to be lucky to get a shot of them; in Nairobi we took a photograph of a stuffed one.

"Ostrich at 9 o'clock," Ben said. "It's a male —they are black and white."

The largest living bird didn't wait to have his picture taken either as he quickly turned to leave. But a group of the most graceful of all antelopes—the impala—obliged. Normally, these animals, intensely alert giving a high-pitched "sneezing" alarm depart rapidly in a series of graceful leaps and bounds; they are considered to be the finest jumpers in all of Africa—far better than the famed springbok of South Africa.

These were young males, distinguished by the lyre-shaped ridged horns, who often live together prior to obtaining their own harem of females.

"How can you tell an impala from a gazelle?" someone asked. "I can't get them straight."

Silently I agreed. It almost seemed as if you couldn't tell the players without a scorecard. Ben explained, "The impala has a prominent *black* streak on either side of a white rump while the gazelle is striped black on its sides. So don't look at their faces—look at their sides or their rear ends."

"Did you know there are two types of zebras?" I asked, paging through the animal guide. "I thought a zebra was a zebra."

"Burchell's is the most common one," Ben answered, "let's see if we can find some, so I can explain the difference. Everyone finished photographing the impala?"

All heads nodded.

"O.K. Let's go. After that, we'll stop for a cold drink from the cooler in the back."

"That might be more enticing than the zebras," I blurted out. Three hours behind a camera lens had taken its toll.

Soon we spotted a restless group of zebras. "See how broad the stripes are on the rump," Ben noted, "that's how you can tell they are Burchell's zebra. The Grevy's zebra are lovelier and taller with narrow, black stripes. I don't know if we

No wonder these Burchell's zebra are skiddish, they are the lion's favorite dish.

will see any Grevy's here; they usually live more north."

Note: there has been much concern about the poaching of the beautiful Grevy's zebra; in the early 1970's there were at least 15,000 in Kenya, but by mid-1977 the total had dropped to below 1,000.

These horse-like creatures nervously watched as we clicked, clicked our cameras.

Finally, we reached the rest spot where we could get out to stretch our legs and have cold drinks. (One of the joys of the trip was the coolness of what was in the cooler. Everyday it was stocked for us.)

"Did you know the zebra is prone to heart attacks and that's why they've never been tamed for beasts of burden?" Ben asked.

I wondered why they felt so stressed, almost like modern man, until I discovered they were the lion's favorite prey.

Note: we were constantly assimilating "new" information and experiences throughout the trip. Another new one occured at bedtime our first night in Meru.

AFTER A DELICIOUS FIVE-COURSE DINNER, we walked back to the room under what seemed like all the stars in the heavens to be greeted with beds encased in mosquito netting.

"This looks like a scene out of a Humphrey Bogart movie," I said laughingly.

"There must be some need for having them," Fred answered thoughtfully.

And there was.

A tip: bring a small mosquito bomb to fog the room, even if netting is available. There aren't many of them but even one can be pesky to sleep with.

Still, I liked the ingenious way the netting was made. There are three ties on the outside allowing you to enter, and three ties on the inside to button-up the hatches.

LIONS ARE WHAT MOST WANT TO SEE in Africa. And we were no different. Both the morning and afternoon game drives hadn't yielded a one. So the group was eager to "get a lion."

Yet, on the last afternoon in Meru, we opted to stay at the Lodge relaxing when they set off; we were tired, perhaps from the lack of sleep at the Ark or was it a thinning of the blood from the dry heat, and altitude? I didn't know.

Noticing the group had returned early to the Lodge, some looking rather peaked (or green around the gills, if you don't mind a fine cliche), I asked, "How was the game drive? Did you see any lions?"

"Did we ever!" they said excitedly. "We coaxed the driver to turn off the road into the bush when a lioness guarding her cubs was spotted. And guess what happened? We got stuck! The driver spun and spun the wheels but that just dug us deeper into the sandy soil. And all this time, we were only 10 yards away from the lioness.

"What did the lioness do?" I asked, just as excitedly.

"Nothing. She just watched us, probably thinking what dumb tourists."

"Then what happened?"

"We couldn't get out of the van as she was too close for comfort. And when she did move away with her cubs, we didn't have a shovel to dig us out. I had visions of spending the night there. But luckily, a lovely family from Nairobi, who were camping in the area, happened along, saw us and stopped. They had a shovel. Whew! I need a—."

(Later I learned that on the way back to the Lodge the lioness was close to the road, and they watched her nurse the cubs. Also, they made a stop at the enclosure where the white rhinos, recently introduced into this park—the only one in Kenya to have these creatures—were kept.)

THE BATTERED, full of static wireless had informed Ben the plane was due to arrive at 10:15 A.M. (There are no phones in many parts of Kenya, so the wireless is the only source of communication.) We were sorry to leave Meru and the Lodge with its yellow hibiscus and fragrant frangipani growing in the courtyard. Yet, I was excited—what new adventure awaited us in Marsabit, the former home of Ahmed?

4 / Marsabit and the Rampaging Lions

THE TITLE in the Kenyan newspaper read:

RAMPAGING LIONS KILLED

The article said two man-eating lions had attacked three people in Marsabit town the day before we left on safari.

I mused on this jolly news while waiting for the plane to be refueled by hand, using a strainer to filter the gas. Too, I wondered if the others had seen the article, but I decided not to mention it, at least at this time.

Marsabit is located almost 400 miles from Nairobi in what's called the Northern Frontier, a wild and woolly spot near the borders of Ethiopia and Somalia. It's the kind of place where the African version of *High Noon* could be filmed—OK Corral and all.

Once airborne, we spotted the unpaved road to Marsabit, running straight like a ramrod north to Ethiopia through the desert wilderness strewn with black lava-rock boulders. The terrain looked parched and inhospitable with ominous volcanic mountains pushed up by the Great Rift fault.

During the course of the safari we were to cross and re-cross this cataclysmic fault which is thousands of miles long, dividing the African continent from Ethiopia's Red Sea to Rhodesia's Zambesi River; elevation ranges from 1300 feet below sea level (the floor of the Dead Sea) to 6,000 feet above sea level with sheer cliffs several thousand feet dropping to the valley floor below.

I gather if you go by van to the Northern Frontier, the top hatch has to be closed, the reddish dust is so thick. I wonder what you do if you have a mechanical breakdown.

Yet, I had heard that Marsabit National

The Great Rift fault seen from the air.

The Kaisut Desert is not the type of place you'd like to be stranded in.

Reserve, an area of some 800 square miles, consisted of forested Marsabit Mountain (there are no "jungles" in Kenya; the Tarzan movies were written by someone who had never been to East Africa), which rises like an oasis out of the desert. And it was true. A dark green patch of trees appeared and Captain Bird buzzed Marsabit Safari Lodge, perched on the edge of a volcanic crater, peeking out amidst the trees.

Waiting for us on the rock-cleared airstrip was Group B, surrounded by a throng of Boran women and children selling hand-made jewelry; these entrepeneurs descended on us like locusts on arrival.

MARSABIT SAFARI LODGE, another newly opened government facility, has the feel of a mountain hunting lodge with large picture windows and rooms connected in a row, motel fashion, thus differing from Meru's boma design.

In the past, travelers who wanted to experience Marsabit had to stay at a privately-run tenting camp (see Kathryn Hulme's amusing account of her stay here in *Look a Lion in the Eye*) or bring their own camping equipment.

Wide windows overlook the water hole.

An elephant show like a trained circus performance greeted our arrival at the Lodge. Pulling up a semi-circle of chairs to watch, elephants arrived and departed for their mud-bath in the water hole, which I learned was the guests' shower water feeding into the green crater directly below the Lodge. Remember this area is noted as the breeding ground of huge elephants, like Ahmed, who was protected when alive by presidential decree, and had a private game warden assigned to protect him from poachers. (The poachers come in from Somalia and are a constant hazard.)

Snorts, trumpeting, the flapping of ears, trunks and tails assailed our eyes and ears. Part of the African experience are the sounds made by the animals which no author can describe fully or even well to the reader—you just have to go to hear them for yourself.

I've always liked the trunk of the elephant—it's like a hand—the tip, highly sensitive to touch can "feel" delicate objects with precision, it's used for food gathering (they eat 300-500 pounds of vegetation/day), breathing, smell, and when crossing deep water, a snorkel.

"When do we eat?" someone said. "I'm starving!"

Again lunch, especially the Kenyan Highland blue cheese on crackers for dessert, was delicious. All the meals throughout the trip were a marvel when I began to think about it—all food has to be flown or trucked into every lodge.

Elephants need mud-baths . . . to protect their bodies from insect bites.

(We ate everything, including unpeeled vegetables, and not a soul was sick.)

"LOOK AT THE BUTTERFLIES—they are everywhere!" Fred said.

"They are lovely. I wonder what kind they are. They almost look like a Monarch, but I'm not a lepidopterist. Maybe Ben knows. Let's ask him."

But he didn't know either. Yet, he informed us that he wasn't surprised to find something unusual in this area—it was noted for the unique in birds and animals like Ahmed or the greater kudu, a rare striped antelope. Now, however, much of the game had disappeared because the area was suffering from a drought that had already lasted 4 years.

I had never experienced a drought before—but it was everywhere. Marsabit Mountain's "rain" forest now was dripping in dust. It looked as if a poor housekeeper lived there.

With every breath of wind, reddish topsoil covered everything, including us. Pictures I had seen of the dust bowl of the 30's began to have real-life meaning.

But the full impact of the drought came on the afternoon game drive to Lake Paradise. This crater lake, made famous through the writings and photography of Martin and Osa Johnson, at one time teemed with wildlife, but now it was barren, barely green, emptied of water and life.

Due to a drought of four years, Lake Paradise is dried up.

The view of dried-up Lake Paradise was sobering.

Standing on the crater's rim, I soberly reflected on man's need for water. Even now the elephants were forced to resort to the lodge's soapy dish and shower water.

Note: I've had reports recently that Samburu has received quite a bit of rain, and hopefully this area has too.

Too, driving down the backside of 5,000 foot Marsabit Mountain to the lake was an unforgettable experience. The washboard road filled with massive boulders was like a steep stairway, pitched so treacherously that we held on to the front seats to protect us from falling on our faces and to soften the sledgehammer jolts of the Land Rover's movements. It took about an hour to go a distance of less than five miles.

My knuckles were white by the time we reached the lake.

Someone asked incredulously, "We're not going back the same way we came, are we?"

Ben didn't answer. Perhaps he wanted to keep us in suspense. A slight grin played across his face before he began to laugh. "No, first we will descend into the lake's floor. There are some really big elephants living there still, like Abdul, the successor to Ahmed. Then we will circle back looking for game along the way—perhaps we'll see a greater kudu—to the road we came in on from the airstrip, which by the way was just built when the lodge opened; otherwise, the road we were on was the only way up the mountain."

Perhaps, I thought, we would have "lost" some members of the group, including me, if *that* road had been our only route during the two-day stay; still, on an one-time-around ride, it was thrilling.

Driving into the lake bed, three solitary bulls were spotted in the distance. "Abdul?" someone asked expectantly.

Ben frowned, examining them through the binoculars. "No. Sorry. My last group was fortunate to get a look at him. But this time, he doesn't seem to be around. Maybe it's the drought."

We were disappointed. Silently, we scanned the forest clearing, but there was only evidences of the drought. No birds sang. No monkeys jumped from limb to limb. Silence prevailed.

I felt as if we had landed on the moon.

A sense of unreality pervaded the remainder

of the day too. On the game drive in the Kaisut desert, we stopped on a high ridge to observe the lunar landscape. Then a scene out of Biblical times appeared. "I can hardly believe it," Fred said quietly, shaking his head. "It looks like Mary and Joseph on their way to Bethlehem."

"Can I have the binoculars?" I asked. "Yes, she's riding the donkey and he's leading it. They look tired and hot. See how she's hunched over, maybe she's pregnant too."

Fred nodded. The others were watching them too as they slowly proceeded toward us.

"They see us," someone said excitedly.

"Yes, they are Samburus," Ben answered.

"They're too far away to get a good shot."

"They won't want to have their picture taken," Ben added, "and we shouldn't photograph them without permission."

Sure enough. She pulled the black shawl over her head, and they changed course, moving off to the left.

About five minutes later, two jewelry encrusted bare-breasted Samburu women stopped the Land Rover, holding up one finger, meaning one shilling for their picture. Since Ben's vehicle wasn't in sight, we decided not to chance this transaction on our own.

Still, this was unreal too. These Africans looked as if they had stepped out of an old *National Geographic.*

Another *Geographic* perfect picture was the rare smallish antelope called a klipspringer, which stands on the very tips of its toes, large shaggy tipped ears pointed forward. Seen perched on the top of a high escarpment ledge, this animal looked as if he was posing for us.

Also, the African night at Marsabit touched on the unreal to scary. It was *so* dark—almost Halloweenish. Maybe my mind is playing tricks on me, I thought. And what about those man-eating lions? No one had spoken of them. Was this another of those "sensational" articles? Tomorrow I said to myself, I'm going to find out.

The ranger's light guided us to our rooms. Closing the door and bolting it tightly, I said to Fred, "*What's* that noise?"

A distinct munching could be heard. Slowly it advanced on the picture window. Peering out I saw a huge dark shape not more than 10 feet away.

"Elephant," Fred said.

(Note: the elephant eats 16 hours/day stripping bark and vegetation from the trees. He's even able to climb a steep embankment such as the one in front of the Lodge to the top of the crater rim in order to forage for food.)

I pulled the covers tightly over my head before going to sleep.

THE NEXT DAY, THE ITINERARY listed: drive down to the desert to visit a Boran village, followed by a visit to the "singing wells."

That was for the morning. Since game was scarce, what about the afternoon? Or better yet, what about the man-eating lions?

Duba, the teenage African engaged to

Duba, the Boran guide.

facilitate our visit to the Borans was standing nearby, so I said, "I hear you had some lions who were man-eaters in Marsabit recently. What's the story?"

He shrugged his shoulders. "Yes, he answered, "they caused quite a stir. And people were hurt."

Overhearing our conversation, the doctor in the group asked, "How badly were the people injured?"

Duba shook his head. "I'm not sure. Maybe one woman lost her leg when the lion attacked her in the kitchen. The others—I don't know—." He paused, lowering his voice, "Maybe you'd like to visit them in the hospital this afternoon and see for yourself?" he asked brightly.

The doctor was delighted.

So, part of the afternoon was settled. Also, another game drive was decided upon—game or no game—as was a visit to the town market. Who knows what the shoppers would uncover there.

I was surprised at Duba's calmness concerning the man-eaters. It appeared as if they were an everyday occurrence. Later, he explained that everyone was afraid of this type of lion in that they were taught by their mother to enjoy a human feast. It seems that man-eaters are *made* not born. Usually it begins when the mother is out looking for food and she chances on a villager guarding the cattle stockade. Instead of killing a cow for dinner, she attacks the man thus finding out that humanity can be tasty. This manner of dining is subsequently transferred to the cubs, who grow up to be man-eaters too. So the game warden has to track the spoor (feces) of the lioness back to the pride, and kill the remaining family.

Whew! I said to myself.

A VISIT TO AN AFRICAN VILLAGE might not sound exciting or even interesting to some. Yet, a glimpse into any country's culture, be it Kenya or France, can prove to be a trip highlight. And so it was for us.

A word about the Kenyan tribes: there are 43 listed, the Kikuyu being the largest with over 2 million and the Elmolo of 200 individuals, the smallest, with the Boran somewhere in between (about 34,000 members).

But the statistics don't show the diversity between each group, as each has their own traditions and boundary lines—and at times, a Hatfield and McCoy mentality has reigned. Duba, for example, saw his parents killed in a tribal war with the Rendilles.

Other traditions can come into play too, causing a schism between the groups. Discussing this, Ben explained, "A Luo man never serves himself straight from the pot—that's a woman's job. Even if the woman is working late in the fields, she will place her husband's food above the door inside the hut. So if a Luo marries a member of a tribe who does not have this custom, marital discord can and usually does occur."

I answered, "Intermarriage is one of the ways to break down tribal distrust. In America, we have Swedes marrying Germans and sharing their customs, not fighting over them—that's why we're called a melting pot of a nation. I believe it's one of the secrets of America's strength."

Ben was thoughtful for a long time. Then he said, "I'm going to take a second wife soon, according to our customs. But she'll be a Luo. I just couldn't—."

Perhaps your children and their children will, I thought.

THE BORAN VILLAGE was located about half a mile out of Marsabit town. The twenty-nine-year-old chieftain was awaiting our visit. And so was everyone else. Youngsters crowded around us selling handmade articles. Beaded gourds and shining copper, brass and aluminum bracelets were offered at reasonable prices. Bargaining began in earnest; I purchased three beautiful bracelets made of copper tubing and steel that had been discarded and now was being recycled.

There are over 600 Borans living in this area. They are a tribe of Hamitic origin, meaning they are descended from the Biblical sons of Ham and were probably one of the earliest major ethnic groups to have entered Kenya. Tall, lanky in build with fine sculptured features they have adapted well to their desert environment, leading a pastoral life.

Some have said the Borans are a fierce tribe but we encountered just the opposite. The chief was wise and friendly and young by our standards to have been elected by the council of elders to such a high tribal office. He invited us into his thatched hut to meet his wife and family.

Inside the hut, a charcoal fire warmed a carved cradle, the bedroom was hung with a beaded

The Boran chieftain poses for a family photo. Notice the spear.

wall hanging and the rooms were as neat as a pin, although they lacked windows. The chief introduced us to his demure and lovely wife, and we asked if they would pose for a photograph.

The doctor in the group whispered to me, "Did you notice he has leprosy in his eyes?"

"Really! No," I said, my interest quickening.

"Yes. I talked to him about it and he said he's planning on going into the hospital soon to take the cure."

I felt relieved, yet saddened that this dread disease still existed in this part of the world.

The chief's wife was adorned with aluminum jewelry.

The Boran chieftan was charming and handsome.

THE SINGING WELLS have been described as an enactment of Old Testament times where herds of goats and cattle are watered and women do the family wash. But to see them is something else.

There is more than one well, each owned by a group of families and twice a week a man's herd is watered but only at the well that belongs to his tribal group. So this meant two things: the cattle were terribly thirsty from a schedule of a drink twice a week; and the families jealously guard their wells allowing only their family members to use them. And for us, it meant we couldn't photograph at will unless we wanted to pay 5 or 6 families a sum for each well.

Standing on the ridge overlooking the braying bovine mass, Ben said, "I'll negotiate. Stay here. I'll see what they want."

The Africans didn't look very friendly. Looking through the binoculars, someone said, "That old man picked up a rock and is waving it at us. What's the matter? I'm not photographing him."

Ben had just returned and told us that the tribesmen don't know the difference between a pair of binoculars and a camera. So it would be best if we put everything away on the walk down the steep incline to the family at the well that would allow us to take pictures.

"What are they charging?" someone asked inquisitively.

For the first (and last) time Ben looked angry. "That family," he said pointing to the old man still holding the rock, "wanted 200 shillings, over $20. And that's ridiculous! The other group wants less, about 120 shillings. Is that O.K.?"

Although we felt "royally" ripped-off, it was a once in a lifetime experience, so everyone agreed, meaning they would pay their share of the expense to Ben after he handed over the

The singing wells are at the bottom of this steep hill.

money from his own pocket. (Note: the cost of photographing the Borans was only 50 shillings and payment was done discretly without a lot of hassle).

My throat felt dry, and my hands were clammy on the descent to the selected well. Would the others stone us?

Sullenly they watched us pass within ten feet without creating an incident. I breathed a sigh of relief, as did everyone else.

These pits supplied by a natural underground stream are called "singing wells" because the Africans chant as they lift the water in a three-stage stepwise fashion from a depth of at least twenty feet. What you look at is a human water-wheel or in some ways, a fire brigade as they pass the bucket down empty to be filled and brought up to the cattle trough above, singing as they work. At times, for a few rounds, the leader will step up the cadence and buckets fly up and down with amazing speed; then the workers break out in wild laughter at the end.

Look at the different levels in the "singing wells."

The youngsters were like those everywhere—friendly.

The scene was mesmerizing. And I almost forgot to take pictures. At this price, I better get moving, I said to myself. So the photographing of the dark bodies against the copper earth began.

A camera tip: the location of the wells causes you to shoot into the morning sun. This causes unpleasant shadows on the Africans' faces. Ask them, especially the children, to move sideways or to face into the sun in order to get better shots.

Walking back to the Land Rover up the precipitous incline, I noticed on the hill's crest herd after herd of cattle still waiting for a drink. It was a wonder they did not stampede the troughs. But by some unknown force or tradition they knew the timing wasn't right—it wasn't their turn.

My knees were rather weak as we bounced back to the Lodge for lunch. I needed a drink too.

MARSABIT TOWN is straight out of Dinesen's *Out of Africa* with its tin-roofed shacks and dirt roads; in fact, it's the essence of Nairobi in years gone by.

Open-stalls dot the narrow market place and I made a list of what produce was being sold:

Some of the humpbacked cattle waiting their turn for water.

peppers, potatoes, charcoal, cabbage, tea, tobacco, coffee beans, tomatoes, curry powder, incense (used as a bug repellent), milk and salt. There even was a blacksmith selling hand wrought knives and spears—fine decorative items for a hunting lodge or cabin wall. Someone in the group purchased a spear for that very purpose.

In the town, we recognized many of the Borans from the village, and some came up to talk. The brightness of 15 year-old Duba was unusual too. With good schooling, he could, perhaps become a leader in the area.

Too, the afternoon game drive on the rough rock-strewn road leading to Lake Turkana yielded some interesting specimens: a female black-bellied bustard; a gerenuk; and many camels belonging to the Rendilles. (This tribe only keeps camels which eat the thornbush, thus allowing them to live peaceably, side by side with the Samburus who only have cattle.)

Feeling tired, Fred and I decided to forgo the visit to Marsabit Hospital. Although there was no assurance they would be allowed to visit, four of the group decided to chance it. They were warmly received in the small hospital which was described as dating back to the early 1900's. And they met the individuals involved in the lion attack which began at 7:30 A.M. when the lioness walked through the open front door of a house where two women were preparing breakfast. One woman managed to escape without serious injuries but the other had to have her leg amputated and her hands were badly clawed. The lioness then went berserk when she discovered she had been locked in, demolishing everything in her path; the game warden shot her.

Later, others heard screams and rushed out to discover a male lion attacking a man, a few hundred yards away from the first incident. People wielding spears, sticks and stones killed this man-eater. But the hands of this man had been badly clawed too, and our doctor wondered if either the man or the woman would ever regain the use of them.

After that, I heard an interesting lion story: it seems that in the early days of building the

A bustard slowly walks away from the camera.

A camel feeds on a tasty tidbit in the desert. Notice the eyelashes.

railroad in Kenya, 28 coolie laborers were eaten by two man-eating lions. It was awful as nobody knew when they would seize someone—asleep or on the job—and drag them into the bush; the bones of the individual being eaten usually were crunched by the man-eaters and this could be heard. So when the engineer in charge, a man by the name of Patterson finally shot the two lions, 28 days apart, there was much rejoicing, and the railroad from Mombasa inland could then be completed.

THE NEXT DAY, as we left the mahogany forest of Marsabit, I reflected on the slice of life we had encountered. From Lake Paradise to the village to the wells, we had experienced much. Perhaps it wasn't so different after all. In fact, I had begun to feel slightly at home.

The road leading out of forested Marsabit National Reserve.

5 / Samburu Lodge, Luxury in the Bush

ONE OF THE MOST BEAUTIFUL and luxurious of all the game lodges—Samburu—is located in the Samburu-Isiolo Game Reserves, 213 miles from Nairobi. Group B, awaiting our 50 minute flight from Marsabit, excitedly told us about our accommodations for the upcoming two nights: the bathrooms are sparkling, so you can wash your hair; the rooms are lovely with a fine view; the food is very good and the bar is great; try the swimming pool, it's wonderful; and bring lots of money for the gift shop, it's well stocked.

Samburu Lodge is a green oasis on the bank of this river—the Uaso Nyiro.

Still, I noticed a frown on one face, so I asked her what she thought. "Didn't like it. Too touristy. Give me the 'bush' anyday," she said.

Oh, well, you can't please all of the people all of the time, I thought.

Located on the banks of the palm-lined Uaso Nyiro River, Samburu Game Lodge with its A-frame thatched roofs, polished wood, wrought iron and waxed brick floors could be a Rockresort (it's under the same management as the New Stanley; a well-run Block Hotel) as it's a place where you could spend a week enjoying the best of both worlds—creature comforts, and the African bush.

Immediately, we noticed things were different here: first, the pace was much busier with groups of tourists congregating everywhere; next, everyone seemed well-dressed compared to us, the veteran but terribly dusty travelers (note: attire is more formal here — some guests wore

Our rooms were in the lovely wing off the main Lodge.

Soaring thatched roofs, like inverted conch shells, add grace and beauty to the Lodge.

The dining room is open on one side giving you a panoramic view of the river.

"Do you have food for me too?" the baby seems to be asking as the mother begs for a handout.

long skirts to dinner); and lastly, underfoot, animals like the vervet monkey hopped noisily about, begging a handout. These creatures can be nasty, causing a bad bite. And the management has posted signs telling the guests that they can get into the rooms if you leave the windows open, and "raid" the place.

All in all, after two days in remote Marsabit, I felt a bit bewildered—as if I *had* come back from the moon.

While waiting for the room assignment, we explored the huge circular bar built on pillars directly over the river bank, where crocodiles float like discarded logs. At night, the crocodiles are fed food scraps while tourists, three deep, attempt to photograph them. Also, across from the bar and dining room is a tree hung with bait to attract a leopard, thus providing what might be deemed a "floor-show" for the guests.

But what excited me the most was the

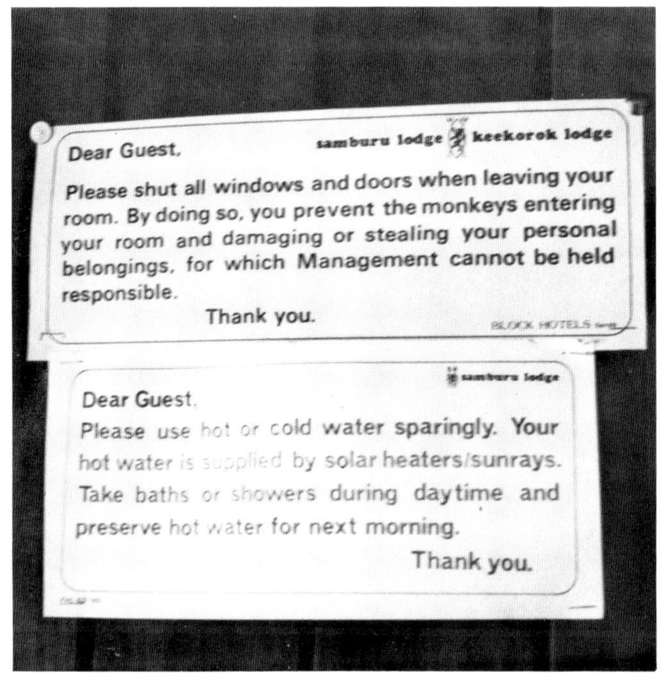

Two signs: one about the monkeys and the other about solar energy.

Signs are posted everywhere to protect the guests.

prevalence of the golden palm-weavers, an orangish-yellow finch-like bird, fluttering everywhere—from coffee cups to drink glasses—like golden butterflies.

Group B was right about the bathrooms, but they failed to mention that the rooms were large with lovely hand screened yellow fabric, rattan furniture, picture windows, and whitewashed walls meeting mahogany ceilings. Too, each room had a balcony where you could sit and read or watch the animals like the Marabou stork, feed on frogs in the river.

I knew I was going to like it here.

In the lovely rooms, mosquito netting is hung from the lights.

This bar has an atmosphere all its own.

The sign says "Stay in Your Car" or . . .

THE ARID TERRAIN of this game reserve (note: a reserve is different from a national park in that tribes live alongside of the animals), really two reserves, Samburu (40 square miles) and Isiolo (75 square miles), back to back and joined by a common 10-mile river frontage, is similar to Meru's with Y-branched doum palms and spike-like thornbush.

But somehow a different atmosphere prevails here. Maybe it's because of these salient features: 30 to 40 foot high termite hills looking like the jolly giant's sandcastles; the detailed and at times humorous roadsigns; the bleached out and sad-looking animal carcasses; and the awesome presence of the Mathews mountain range on the horizon.

"Hurry up, everyone. Hurry!" Ben admonished the group. "Lions. Two of them have been spotted not more than a quarter of a mile from here. We want to be the first to get there. Now where did our driver go?" (Since we flew into

you might be the next carcass on the landscape.

Huge 30 foot high termite hills dot the landscape.

each lodge, two vehicles—I've called them Land Rovers for consistency throughout the book—but they ranged from vans to Toyotas, were put at our disposal for the length of each stay; this worked out well.)

"*Twende* (let's go)!" Ben instructed the grinning driver in Swahili who climbed into the front seat as if nothing was the matter.

"*Ndiyo bwana* (yes, sir)!" said the driver, his head bobbing up and down in agreement.

"*Harambee* (let's all pull together)!" Ben answered sternly.

"Yes, *harambee*," Fred and our doctor said in unison. They smiled at each other as they had been studying Swahili together on off times during the trip.

"*Haya* (O.K.)," the driver said laughingly.

By now everyone was smiling.

In a matter of minutes, we came upon two lionesses stretched out alongside the road taking an afternoon siesta in the shade. Flies covered their muzzles and necks. One was sleepier than the other. Suddenly four other vans converged on the twosome, surrounding them.

The more alert one watched the shiny vehicles with the funny people inside taking

The lioness was surrounded by vans.

Notice how close the lionesses are to the road.

photograph after photograph, but she didn't move a muscle.

I was happy we had arrived first as we had the front view of the pair—much to the dismay of the other vehicles. Quickly I used my telephoto lens and as I was about to switch to another, two more vans arrived in a plume of dust. I felt as if a war party of Indians had swooped in to capture the settlement.

Then it became evident something or better yet, someone van—meaning us—had to give up their ringside seat to the others. We moved off. Still, the lionesses didn't move.

Someone said, "Darn, those were *our* lionesses. Why did the others have to spoil the fun?"

I agreed.

But Ben said, "Don't worry, we'll see more lions. Maybe a leopard or even a cheetah. There's plenty of game in Samburu. Just wait and see."

We only felt *slightly* appeased. Maybe it was because we were half-way through the safari and had become quite seasoned travelers who desired to see and do as much as possible. Or perhaps it was due to the fact that few, if any traveler, gets enough of the mysterious power of *simba.*

And, we discovered, during the remainder of the stay at Samburu, that Ben was right. There was a myriad of game in this small reserve (an ornithologist friend who goes to Africa two times a year told me that there used to be even *more* game here than there is now). The *Field Guide to the National Parks of East Africa*—another good book to have along—listed close to 90 mammals, many like the dik-dik or gerenuk we had never seen, and almost 400 birds in Samburu.

Samburu may be small but it is beautiful. The Mathews mountain range is in the distance.

A LARGE FLOCK OF VULTURINE GUINEA FOWL—a game bird with a white streaked neck and brilliant cobalt blue plummage—took our minds off the lions almost immediately as they crackled like turkeys on the way to the river.

The popularity of the river can't be underestimated in this reserve. Over the course of two days, we were to ford and reford this sustainer of life—the one necessity lacking in Marsabit. All along the river bank the five-foot-tall Marabou stork, a very large scavenger that associates with vultures, is seen, its conspicuous air-filled pouch dangling from a pink neck. Silently they lift one leg and then the other almost like a group of old men in morning coats waiting for some unknown event. Some people dislike them and call them "dirty" old men or "undertakers," because they eat carrion like the vulture, but upon reflection, they appeared rather sad, perhaps maligned as they perform a

Looking like penguins, the Marabou stork feeds on the sandbar.

The vulturine guinea fowl is a brilliant blue.

The saddle-bill stork's bill is like a neon sign—red, black and yellow.

Elephant at 11 o'clock.

good function too—that of destroying locusts, when necessary.

And we were fortunate to encounter the rare 5½ foot black and white saddle-bill stork whose red, black and yellow bill set off a chorus of "Oh's and Ah's."

Even the secretary bird perched on top of the acacia trees was appreciated.

OTHER ANIMALS vied for our attention too. Like the pachyderm at 11 o'clock, unfurling his ears as a deterrent to our approach. Also, the ears function in much the same way as a radiator with the blood leaving the surface ear vessels several degrees cooler than the incoming fluid.

Too, the skin of the elephant particularly intrigued me. It is an inch thick in places with the characteristic wrinkling being an asset for cooling the increased surface area. Close examination

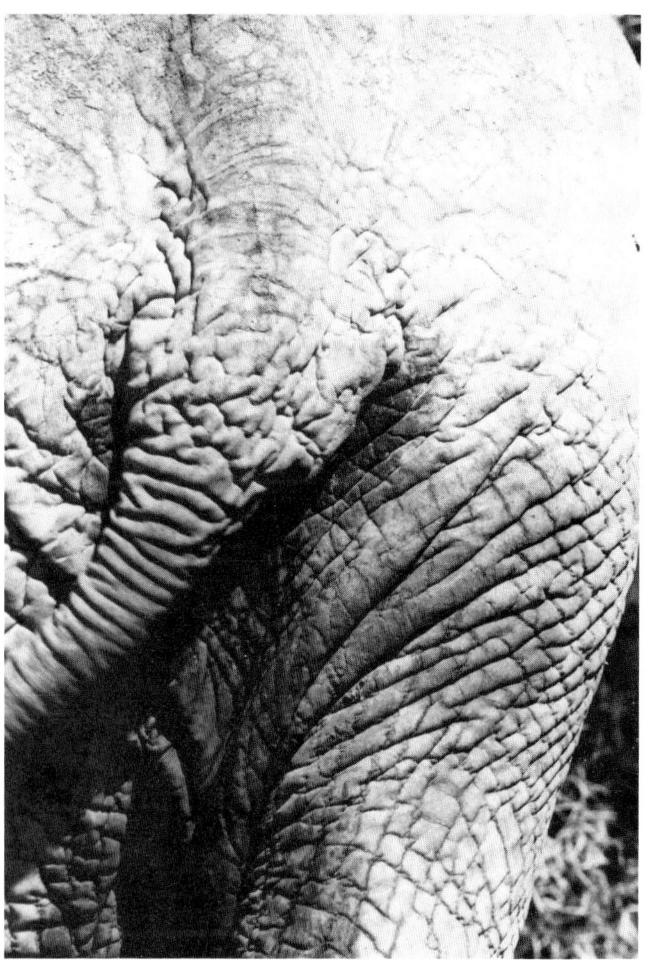

Wonder if Elizabeth Arden could do anything with these wrinkles?

of the elephant's hide would show it's covered with bristle-like hairs. And the long black hairs at the tip of the tail are often made into bracelets which are said to bring the wearer luck, although I don't believe such a story. In Nairobi, I noticed gullible tourists buying plastic bracelets sold by street vendors as the "real" thing.

By the end of the afternoon, we had visually drunk-in and photographed more animals than we had almost seen on the whole trip. Especially interesting was a solitary bull waterbuck with his gracefully curved horns, and a small group of young rams congregating around a favorite tree almost as if they were swapping local gossip.

Another animal we had never heard of but which we thought unique was the 3 foot gerenuk, often called a "giraffe-gazelle," due to its extremely long neck. It stands on its hind legs to eat, thus enabling it to reach higher and more tender shoots. Some have written that this animal reminds you of an out-of-proportion "blown glass" ornament. But I didn't think so. They are quite lovely. And I thought, where but in Africa could you find the grace of a gazelle combined with the "genteelness" of a giraffe.

So does the Kenya impala, considered the finest in all of Africa. Notice the stunning lyre-shaped horns and the black-streak on the rump.

The waterbuck has a beautiful "trophy" head.

The gerenuk's long neck helps him to feed on more tasty fare.

A batik showing the grace and beauty of the gerenuk.

"What's that little guy with the ears hiding under that fallen limb?" someone asked. "I've never seen him before."

"A dik-dik," Ben said quietly.

"A what?"

The dik-dik is a small reddish-brown antelope about the size of a hare (15 inches tall or less) that you can't help falling in love with and perhaps would want to take home for a pet. With big brown eyes, and over-sized ears alertly pointed up, they gaze inquisitively at the vans, then they bound away in frisky little hops, only to reappear as if they were playing hide and seek, to get another look at you.

"It's amazing," Ben added, "but they don't need water. They get enough from the foliage they eat to survive."

The dik-dik with the tuft of hair on top of his head is adorable.

Before returning to the lodge, a herd of the tallest and most beautiful of the zebras—the Grevy's zebra—crossed our path. This zebra differs from the Burchell's in that it's taller (as much as 14 hands), the stripes are very narrow and stop at the belly which is snowy white, the legs are finely striped right down to the hoofs, the mane is high extending to the withers, the ears are larger and broader, it brays like a donkey (the Burchell barks), and the face mask is more pronounced.

Note: as I said before in the chapter on Meru, this zebra is almost extinct; it's hide has been made into handbags, telephone directories, watchbands, and even coats. I know of people who now go into shops and complain to the buyer if these goods are sold. Wonderful. Yet, this might not even save this zebra as there is more and more land used for agriculture in East Africa. This means the zebra who provides a valuable role in the ecosystem of grazing on the tougher grass which others like the wildebeest can't eat, will be pushed off the savannah grassland. So maybe the day will come when a child will ask, "What is a zebra?"

So, by the end of the game run, we were immensely satisfied with all we had seen and done; the lions weren't mentioned again.

BEFORE DINNER, many members of the group, including us, headed for the African Heritage boutique located in the lodge's lobby. Stunning batiks, handsome wood sculpture (the elephants and the giraffes are marvelous), Joy Adamson prints, books, even clothing fill the shop. No wonder Group B told us to bring lots of cash when shopping here—there's so much to purchase. But there's one hitch. Sales are cash and carry, meaning if you are a credit conscious American you are out of luck; also it's not possible to put your purchases on the room bill. Maybe, in time, this will change (I hope so). So bring lots of Kenya cash or a personal check. Note: this is a branch of the larger shop on Kenyatta Avenue in Nairobi, so you might want to make your purchases there, although I don't know if they accept credit cards either.

No wonder the Grevy's zebra hides—he's an endangered species in Kenya.

Take a look at the markings of the Grevy's zebra: narrower stripes on the body, all-white belly and striped stocking legs.

Dinner consisted of fresh grapefruit cocktail, hot consomme, grilled steak, french fries, tender green beans, luscious sherry trifle, a selection of fresh fruits, Kenya cheeses with tea or coffee served on the veranda overlooking the river.

A tip: it is helpful to know that in Swahili *chai* is tea, *moto* is hot, so *chai moto* means hot tea and *kahawa* is coffee. If you order iced tea, you might not always get it, but the word for iced is *barafu.*

"Did you see the crocodiles being fed food scraps before dinner?" someone asked as we were about to leave the table. "I got in on the tail end of it," the person added, "and people were three deep taking pictures of the sight."

"Ugh!" someone else shuddered. "Who likes crocodiles? Those ugly jaws filled with teeth scare the life out of me."

"We were there at the beginning of the orgy," I said. "We saw them lumber out of the water and aggressively take the food, making the most *awful* sounds. Frankly, I was too frightened to take any pictures—and anyway at dusk a flash is needed."

"I can't see why they feed them," another added. "What good is a crocodile?"

"It makes a darn good show for the tourists,"the first speaker suggested.

Yes, I thought, it does make for a show that is rare indeed. In fact, when you are at Samburu, find out the feeding time and bring your flash (this is one of the few times on the trip when a flash comes in handy).

Still, the question, What good are crocodiles? haunted me. I discovered later that crocs are an endangered species and in Kenya, the Nile crocodile has been protected since the early 1950's. Kenya's Lake Turkana (formerly Lake Rudolf) is home for 12,000 crocs, making it the world's largest remaining concentration of Nile crocs; poaching does occur but these crocs have bony growths in the hide making them of poor quality for wallets and handbags (there are laws against crocodile items in the U.S. but not in Europe).

Yet, why protect them? What good are they? The answer is that they keep other

A crocodile takes a sun bath on the river bank.

animals, namely fish, from overproducing, and they excrete the food they eat as nutrients for other plants and animals to use. In America, the alligator in the Florida Everglades digs waterholes during the dry season, thus keeping the other animals alive.

So they aren't so bad after all. And if I ever go to Samburu again, I'm going to obtain some good photographs of them—scary teeth and all.

We were almost ready to retire when Fred said, "There's some commotion going on across the river. Let's take the flashlight and go out to see what's going on."

"I bet it's a leopard taking the bait. Hear those sounds."

Excitedly we hurried outdoors. Arc lights illuminated the African blackness. We met others who had heard the noise too, and they whispered that yes, there was an animal growling and tearing at the chained piece of meat.

But it wasn't a leopard—it was a lioness—a tawny body savagely attempting to tear the meat loose to take to her pride. When she discovered she couldn't remove it, she settled down in the crouch of the tree to have dinner herself. I focused in with my telephoto, but the scene was difficult to take, especially from the walkway in front of the rooms. A tip: a veranda seat supplies a better view, so take one and wait until 10 P.M. (at least), if you can, for an animal to arrive.

Just the week before we arrived, a leopard took the bait at noon, offering perfect photo material for the luncheon crowd. But we weren't so fortunate.

Still, the excitement of the hushed group on the walkway was equal to the Ark. In fact, it was the Ark all over again.

THE NEXT DAY, as we approached a baboon troup on the game run, someone asked inquisitively, "Did the baboons keep you awake last night?"

"They sure did," I said, turning around in the front seat to talk. "The screams were awful as if someone was being bludgeoned to death."

"I wanted to get up and throw a shoe at them," someone else chimed in, "but I knew it wouldn't help."

Baboons, it seems, create noise—really hysterical screams—day and night as the large males deal out discipline such as slaps which are more like karate chops, to those lower in the hierarchy. Yet, I wondered why this maniac behavior continued even at night. Perhaps there were females in season or was it due largely to their moody aggressive nature? I didn't know. Still, of all the African animals, they were the ones I liked least.

Suddenly, a female showed a nodule packed pink backside to us.

"Hemorrhoids," said our doctor.

Baboons constantly move about but this sentinel struck a pose for us.

By noon, the searing sun was high in the intensely blue sky. Many animals were sighted and strangely enough we never seemed to tire of any of them—like the elephant herds forming a protective circle around a tiny baby or the long-necked black and white ostrich awkwardly picking his way through the bush.

The flesh-colored thighs of the male ostrich make it look like a Toulouse-Lautrec dancer.

And too, the purpose of a safari is to totally distract you from thinking of anything else.

So we were naturally excited when our driver informed us that cheetahs had been spotted. We had stopped for something out of the wonderful cooler and the other drivers had told him of two cheetahs, presumably on a hunt, a mile away.

The cheetah differs from the leopard in many ways (note: tigers live only in India, not Africa). First, it's not a true cat in that its claws are blunt like a dogs and are only semi-retractable. Its tawny coat is more evenly spotted with a ringed black tail. A characteristic marking is the black "tear" line extending from the corner of the eyes to the jaw. In hunting, the leopard ambushes its prey or drops from trees, while the cheetah, considered the fastest mammal alive, chases it like a greyhound at speeds of 60-70 miles per hour—but it can only maintain this speed for 100 yards or more, so two will hunt together preying on the tiny dik-dik or medium size antelopes. And finally, it will hunt during the day, and therefore is seen far more frequently than the savage leopard which is a night animal.

Mounting a rise, we saw the pair in the distance crossing an open stretch of bush. We almost gasped in unison, they were such a magnificent sight to watch as the rippling sleek

The cheetah has to hunt through thornbush with its spike-like needles—ouch!

bodies searched slowly for prey. Was it a dik-dik or some other antelope they had their eye on? We couldn't tell.

"Oh, no, I'm running out of film," I said, my voice raising two registers.

"So am I," said Fred. "Hand me another one *please.*"

Silently I prayed we wouldn't miss the shot of the year while we changed film. Isn't that always the way when you are in the middle of something stupendous, I thought.

"Can we get closer?" someone asked the driver.

He grinned, gunned the motor and set the van on an unmarked course across the landscape.

"Let's not get stuck," someone else added firmly.

"No, *bwana,*" he answered, giving us another toothy smile. "We follow. No stuck."

The van lurched like a bucking bronco through the thornbush, narrowly missing a few large boulders and a broken axle as we attempted to keep pace with the intent hunters.

Then something moved. In a blink of the eye,

Take a look at the characteristic markings of the cheetah—the black "tear" line under the eye and the all-over spots with a ringed tail.

they were off. All I could see was a tail attached to a body which had chosen its prey, seized its throat, causing death by strangulation. We surmised it was a dik-dik.

No one spoke. A mourning hush had descended over the van.

It was several minutes before someone wondered, if they would chose to dine in front of our noses, or would they remove the carcass. They did the latter, taking the kill down the embankment and across a narrow stretch of the river to a secluded spot we couldn't get to.

Some of us were very disappointed.

The fastest mammal alive makes a kill in a thornbush.

AN AFTERNOON SIESTA was usually in order after lunch. Today we really needed one. Words like deeply contented or even glutted crossed my mind. I went to sleep wondering if anything could ever compare to the almost electrical tension of the morning's hunt.

When Ben informed us that we would try to photograph the native Samburus during the afternoon game run, I was happy. The proud beautiful faces of the Africans were a photographer's delight and too, they were less emotionally taxing than the animals.

The first group that seemed to be waiting for us by the side of the road was a male threesome, speared, magnificently masculine, dressed in

Earrings, headband and necklaces are part of the warriors attire.

Dressed to emphasize their manhood Samburu warriors pose for us.

White x's were painted on the face and cheeks smeared with orange pigment.

orange-red, faces smeared with ochre. Two were young warriors called Morans who look after the surplus herd until they are allowed to marry at age thirty.

A respect for all elders is emphasized in the Samburu culture, and a powerful curse is held over the younger generation by the tribal elders to insure good behavior. So we found them to be friendly and cheerful (and not greedy as far as the price we paid to photograph them).

The Samburu call themselves "the world's top people," for what reason I do not know, but few tribes display such an appreciation for the human body and an ingenious use of eclectic materials for decoration.

The handsome young boy, serious and rather shy, was adorned with a necklace of tiny brown and white shells which equaled the finery of his brothers.

By chance, the next group was a trio of women, again dressed in orange but a lighter shade which beautifully set off their dark skin. The eldest, a narrow cigar clenched between her teeth, appeared to have the two younger ones in tow. Out of the corner of her mouth she bargained with Ben, giving us a half-crooked but pleased smile when she finished.

I was pleased we could take as many shots as we wanted, and when I asked if I could take each one individually, they seemed delighted, especially the shy center one with the dove-like charm on her forehead which was a match to the eldest's (perhaps they were sisters).

After we were on our way again, bouncing

The fine appearance of this boy is seen in the long eyelashes, limbs, and beautifully shaped shaven head.

The leader smoked a cigar and wore long leather earrings.

along, someone said, "Weren't they lovely? So nice."

"Yes," I added, "so far I've been impressed by the sincerity and friendliness of the natives. The waiters want to serve you. And the people want to be photographed, naturally they want the money, but still, there's not a trace of surliness—it's as if they want to please."

"Except for those Africans at the singing wells," the person reminded me.

"True. But that was different. They were the only ones. And Kenya is a land of many tribes—and many faces. Lovely ones, at that."

THE NEXT DAY I counted the number of days remaining on safari. Five. Time had flown. And where had it gone?

As I stood on the balcony watching a group of male impala timidly drink at the edge of the sandbar in the river, Fred said, "A penny for your thoughts."

"Oh," I answered, "I'm laughing at myself for being so skiddish about the safari in Nairobi. The safari hasn't been a hardship *at all.* In fact, it's been a *joy.*"

Fred gave me a hug as he responded heartedly with, "Ditto."

This lovely Samburu girl wears a cross on her headdress.

6/Island Camp, Rest Spot at Lake Baringo

OUR NEXT TWO DAYS were to be spent at an ideal spot for a change of pace and a chance to wind down from all the game viewing —Island Camp, a luxury tented camp located on Ol Kokwe, a small island four miles out in the middle of Lake Baringo, one of Kenya's Rift Valley lakes. This is an ornithological haven with over 400 different species recorded. Island Camp is the brain child of Jonathan Leakey, the son of the famous anthropologists, who also runs a snake farm on the lake.

Our 40 minute flight took us over blue volcanic hills and Samburu's Colcheccio ranch, a lovely new spot complete with tennis courts that was about to be opened. We arrived close to 1 P.M. I had expected the lake to be emerald green or at least blue but a cafe-au-lait appearance was seen from the air. Strange. Later I learned that silt from overgrazing by tribal cattle was seeping into the lake at a rapid rate, thus causing it to turn brown, but this didn't deter the local inhabitants from water-skiing or swimming.

As we disembarked from the air-conditioned

Lake Baringo, one of the Rift Valley lakes, plays host to a luxury tented camp.

craft, we were rudely awakened to the heat—I guessed it was over 100°, but dry, with a wind that blew like a hair dryer set on high. We sought the shade under the aircraft's wings until the Land Rover arrived to transport us to the dock where *The Islander,* a sturdy well-used speed boat was to ferry us on a half-hour's ride to the camp.

In the distance, shimmering like a green South Sea island mirage was Island Camp. Where are the tents? I wondered. All I could see were palm thatched roofs supported by tree stilts.

Visions of grass-skirted Polynesian girls waiting for us with leis floated across my mind—the sun must be getting to me, I thought.

As we docked, I saw that Island Camp is the *ultimate* of hideaways. It's so utterly secluded that even the President of the United States could relax without a bodyguard. And the tents are secluded too—set under a permanent Makuti thatched roof on a concrete slab with your own adjoining shower and toilet. Girl Scout camp was *never* like this.

Under the thatch is a permanent luxury tent looking out over the shimmering lake.

Exclusively remote is Island Camp out in the middle of Lake Baringo.

Blue skies, fluffy white clouds heighten the thatched South Sea Island accommodations.

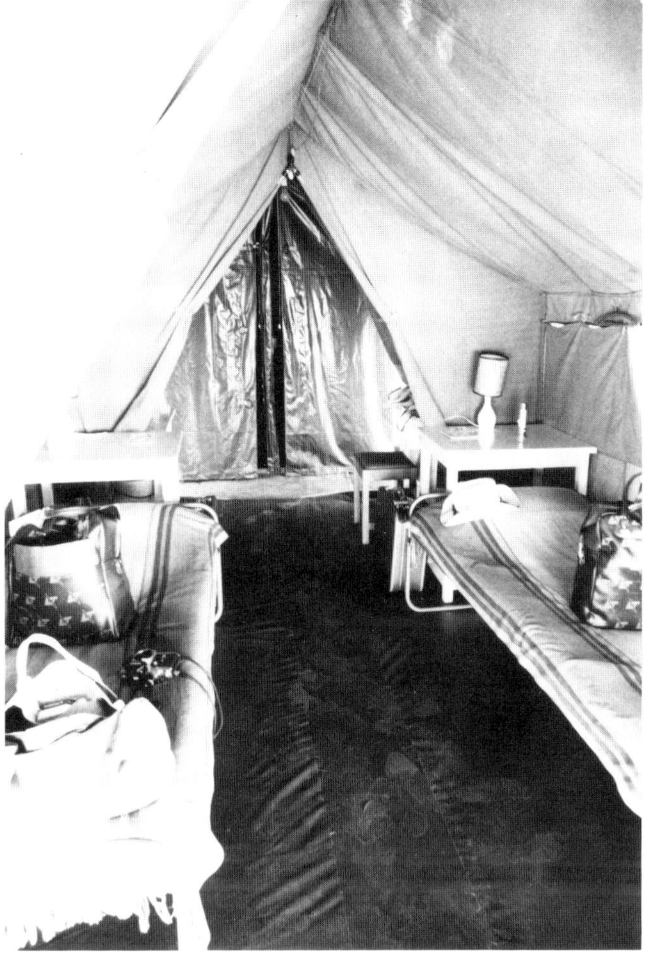

The tent has all the amenities—soft beds, night tables, and an adjoining shower and toilet.

We were met by Lionel Nutter, the manager who in true Marlon Brando style was wearing a blue patterned African skirt. Modestly, he informed us that lunch was waiting for us. And what a lunch! Homemade green pea soup, a yummy lamb stew, fresh peas and carrots and rich chocolate mousse for desert.

"Isn't this place *something?*" someone commented after lunch.

"Sure is. I bet it's the Ritz of tented camps!" another added, shaking his head in wonderment.

"The manager told me that they are going to put in a swimming pool. Imagine!"

I smiled. The place reminded me of a spot on a British Virgin Island called Little Dix Bay. All that was missing was the palm trees.

"Ready to take an afternoon nap?" Fred inquired.

"In a minute," I said, "I'd like to buy a few things in the gift shop first, if you don't mind."

Fred, knowing I'm not much of a shopper except when I really need something or I see a bargain, willingly consented.

The tiny 4 x 6 foot gift shop carried a good assortment of hand-screened African cloth, embroidered cotton tops, some from India, T-shirts, and beautifully made sisal trivets (a useful gift).

"I could sit here all afternoon," Fred said contentedly as I arrived at the tent with my purchases. He was ensconced in a deck chair serenely

The view directly in front of the tent.

enjoying the magnificent view. Shafts of gold pierced the cliff face of a uninhabited island in the lake. Three natives in a homemade boat sailed slowly by.

"What's on the agenda? Did Ben say?"

"It seems the afternoon is free. The Njemps dancers who were supposed to perform for us are indisposed.

"Indisposed with what?"

"Ben says they had a big night last night—meaning too much 'fire water.' So—," Fred said smilingly, raising his eyebrows. "But tomorrow's another day," he added.

"Fine." I answered. "I'm happy to take it easy this afternoon. It's a pleasant change. No baboon or tourist noise. Not even a frog croaking. Aah—peace and quiet."

"Well, there *is* one thing—," Fred said hesitantly.

"What?"

At that minute, a brown furry head came into view, slowly cropping the grass along the side of the tent.

"That!" Fred said, pointing to an immature bushbuck—the camp pet—skillfully utilized as an animal lawnmower.

We laughed.

One of the few animals on the island was this untamed reddish-brown bushbuck.

OL KOKWE MEANS "MEETING PLACE," and it's where the chieftains of the Njemps, a local tribe related (cousins) to the Masai, held their tribal councils. Now on this summit site is the camp's open air bar and restaurant. We met there at 5 P.M. after a billy-goat climb to the top (you need good legs and lungs here). A new "birder" group had arrived led by a portly beaded Swiss, a delightful ornithologist who was on his 22nd trip to Africa. Long lenses (up to 1000 mm) abounded in this group and a babble of United Nations languages rose to a crescendo as they scurried to and fro identifying birds like the small red-capped cardinal woodpecker.

Lionel informed us it was a full house. All eleven tents were in use.

Dressed in the recent gift shop purchases of a sheer mauve top and matching skirt made of African cloth tied (and pinned) around the waist native style, I watched the fiery sun go down and the large African moon come up. Waves lapped against the shore. A cool breeze rushed across the lake. Life can be sweet, I thought.

Dinner again was heavenly: creamy tomato cheese soup, rare roast beef, light cucumber puree, and creme carmel.

After dinner, the ornithologist quietly gave a lecture to his group while we congenially laughed and chatted.

By the time we retired, a very stiff wind had come up and we had to zip up the tent front to prevent objects from toppling over. I was happy the tent was permanently anchored as perhaps we would have floated away like Mary Poppins.

Still, the natural air-conditioning felt good.

Our open-air meeting place. Notice the tripod set-up of the man at the table on the right.

I HAD HEARD MUCH ABOUT THE AFRICAN SUNRISES AND SUNSETS before coming. How they had magic and romance. And it's true. First, there's a glimmer of molten gold, then another dross and another until the sun bursts or sets stupendously over the craggy Rift Valley mountains.

A tip: purchase a star filter and use it when photographing a sunrise or sunset. Remove your skylight filter first, otherwise you could possibly get vignetting.

A word about African breakfasts—they are quite English consisting of: pitchers of orange and grapefruit juice set out buffet style along with bananas, wedges of papaya, cantaloupe and pineapple halves and bowls of cold cereal or oatmeal; eggs and bacon can be ordered.

In case you may think there isn't much to do at Island Camp except eat and relax, quite the opposite is true. There are many excursions available like the island boat trip which takes in magnificent scenery along with bird watching, viewing the many African fish eagles whose white heads and chests with black wings are very striking. We found that this trip was a great change from being cooped up in the Land Rover or van all day. Too, you might want to investigate the legend of a Loch Baringo monster who lives off Gibralter Island, another tumble of rock in the lake; Gibralter is also noted for its colony of the largest of all herons, the red-necked goliath which we saw peacefully floating like 5-foot tall decoys off the island.

But what we immensely enjoyed was going ashore to visit a Njemps village. The Njemps, a lake people, are herdsmen—it's their cattle that are overgrazing the land causing the silt to be deposited in the lake—and they also fish from primitive rafts made of logs lashed together with sisal for big whiskery, delicious eating catfish called *tilapia,* that are smoked over wood fires and then sent in packing cases to posh Nairobi hotels.

The excursion to the Njemps village is by boat.

Smoked fish for dinner? The Njemps are the ones who can provide this request.

A Njemps fisherman builds his primitive craft.

The Njemps are a happy tribe. Notice the affection of the pair on the left.

Two brothers pose for us.

We were greeted by regal-bearing women and smiling, dark-skinned children, darting to and fro.

"Many of the young men," Ben explained "are off tending the almost 1000 head of cattle the Njemps own." He paused for a moment to tell us to look around and take as many pictures as we wanted. As friends of Jonathan Leakey, meaning guests of Island Camp, photography, much to our surprise, was free. An annual lump sum is given to the village by Leakey for posing. Then he added, "Cattle is wealth to the African. And the man who is head of this tribe is wealthy. That's why he's able to take six wives. In fact, he has a total of 36 children—10 are sons, some of whom are married and many of their children you see playing here."

I noticed a laughing family group where one child wearing only a beaded collar was hugging a brother.

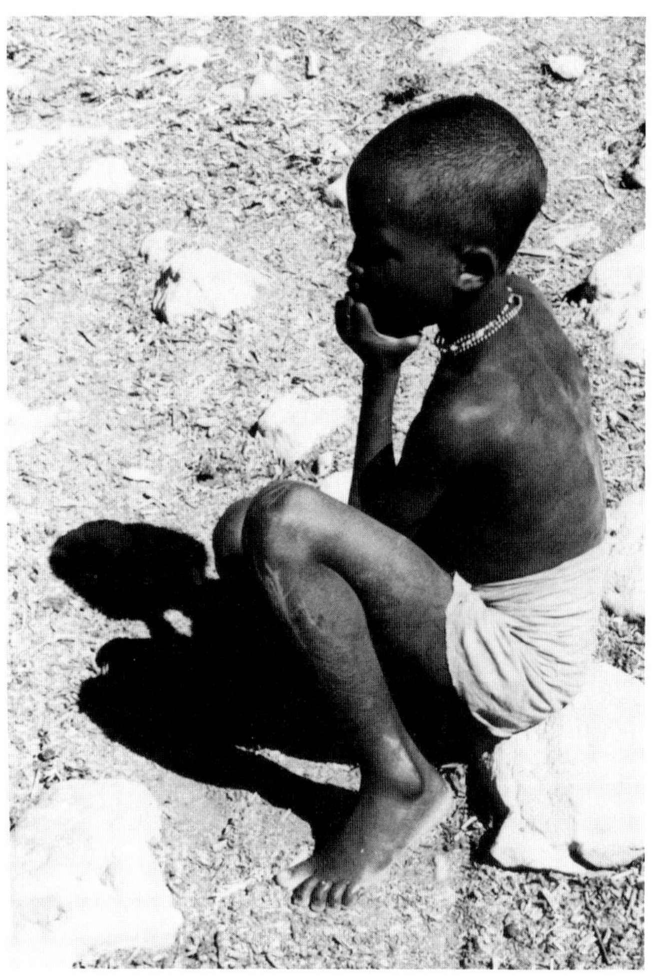

The thinker: Njemps style.

Other children grouped along the shore line were helping with the fishing catch.

Village life has the appearance of a busy day camp, I thought.

As we climbed into the motorboat, someone remarked, "This place is so neat and clean. And just think, for a change, no one was trying to sell us a thing."

True.

BACK AT CAMP, someone asked Ben, "What's on the agenda for this afternoon? I hope it isn't a visit to that snake farm you told us about."

Ben grinned, knowing this excursion, when available, is not too popular. "No, this afternoon a group of Njemps dancers will perform for us. I'm sure they are up to it by now. Tomorrow we'll cross the lake to visit Jonathan's snake farm. But don't feel you have to go if you don't want to. It's really interesting though."

"I'll think about it," the person said. "Snakes and crocodiles aren't my cup of tea."

Someone else interjected, "Mark my words, I bet we'll all end up going because we don't want to miss anything."

A digression to mention a word about the group: we couldn't have hand-picked a better one. I felt I could have a lasting friendship with each person. There were five couples from five different states. Each member with their varied backgrounds and vocations brought something special to the whole; all were world travelers. But I must add, groups can only work well when each person gives more than he or she receives—that's the only way. And ours did.

In the late afternoon, we walked to the cool grassy glade about 300 yards down the steep slope from the main lounge area to see the colorful troup of Njemps dancers perform marriage and warrior dances. A string of canvas chairs were lined up at one end for us to sit in, while the group, greased and speared, dressed in orange-sheet saris lined up at the other end. Some of the shaven-headed women, hands up to their mouths, were already chanting.

Quickly I checked the light to see if there was enough filtering through the acacia treetops to get good telephoto shots; there was. Soon, with a chorus of grunts and shouts from the warriors, the group began to move towards us, spears held high. Their voices rose, louder and louder, to a fever pitch, as they advanced on us. In unison, they dropped their spears into attack position. Again they moved forward. Now the spears were aimed directly at our hearts. They lunged. Someone in our group let out a muffled scream. Others, like myself, were frozen to the chair. But as in any mock battle, they stopped about two feet from us, their serious faces breaking out in smiles at our fright.

By the time they had returned giggling to the

Strange but interesting African dances were performed by a group of Njemps.

A Njemps warrior puts his heart and soul into the dance.

Young Njemps women intently watch their men dance . . .

while dusty feet keep time to the leaping rhythm.

other side of the glade to regroup for another dance, I had regained my wits and remembered the camera in my lap; on this dance, I hadn't taken one shot, missing a golden opportunity. (A tip: the dancers usually perform this attack first, so be ready for a telephoto shot and then a close-up of their faces as they lunge.)

In the next dances, the warriors leaped like jack-in-the-boxes, while the women shouted praises and clapped their hands. When the leaps were especially high, the troup chanted louder as if to applaud the effort. I watched their dusty feet go up and down, up and down, wondering how they could stand it. But they were enjoying themselves immensely. In fact this spring-like leaping can go on for hours as pairs, trios and

The marriage dance is warmly intimate.

quartets compete to see who can leap the highest and longest.

I felt as if I was watching 20 Mexican jumping beans.

After a half an hour of the repetitive dancing, some of us were feeling restless. "Don't they do anything else except jump?" someone asked Ben.

"No," he answered, "that's it."

Yet, I found the dancing to be quite interesting, especially the finale, a marriage ritual, where couples to the sound of the rhythmic human voices swayed, hugged and jumped.

I said to Ben, "It's amazing what they can do without using any instruments. That's what makes the whole thing so—well, so hypnotic."

He nodded.

EVENING WAS THE STUFF OF OLD MOVIES again—the far-away mountains melted into a soft smokey light; a huge African moon sailed up from behind Gibralter Island and millions of stars hung in the sky.

Again I had "gone native" (a tip: this is something you might want to do with the lovely African cloth). And again dinner was five star, as we were treated to creamy cauliflower soup, *tilapia*—the fish of the Njemps—bathed in tomato sauce, barbecued chicken, crispy fresh green beans, tiny new potatoes and not too sweet tapioca pudding for dessert.

After dinner, I asked unflappable Lionel how he managed to run such a tight ship. He said that he had brought his very capable safari cook with him when he arrived almost four years ago, and he is the one who produces the feasts we were having in a small kitchen down the slope, about 50 yards away. Then the hard-working African waiters on winged feet, perhaps made possible by all that jumping, ferry it up to the guests.

Whew! I thought.

We talked late into the night with Lionel who hadn't been off this tiny island for 8 months. I didn't think the beauty of Baringo could hold me for that long. But then I wasn't Lionel with his young manageress—a ravishingly pretty girl.

"WHO IS NOT GOING TO LEAKEY'S SNAKE FARM this morning? Raise your hands," Ben cheerfully said to the group.

Silence.

One person looked down shamefully.

Another looked up as if there was a crack in the sky.

"We're going to leave in a few minutes," Ben continued," so raise your hands now or forever hold your peace."

Ben waited. More silence.

Then he shook his head, looked at his watch, and said, "O.K. We leave in three minutes *exactly*. First, we'll see the flamingos on the east side of the lake, then on to the snake farm." Momentarily he turned away. Then he swung around and said seriously, "Remember, no one has to go who doesn't want to."

When we boarded the boat everyone was present and accounted for. Yesterday's prophecy had been fulfilled—no one wanted to miss a thing.

As the boat skimmed along, I mused on how I wasn't too enthralled to go either. I've been afraid of snakes ever since my last year in college, when as a biology major, I had to share office space with a boa constrictor whose cage was on a shelf directly above my desk. Whenever I entered the lab, I was always scared to death that he'd somehow be out. But happily he rarely moved. Sleepily he watched as I did research on a senior paper entitled, *Parasites in the Blood of Snakes.*

On most itineraries Lake Nakuru to the south is the spot where over a million flamingos, described as the greatest bird spectacle on earth by American ornithologist Roger Tory Peterson, can be seen. Since this was not on our itinerary, I was delighted that a good-sized population of flamingos were breeding on Baringo, thus enabling us to see this pink troup of almost 5 foot tall ballet dancers.

Slowly our boat inched towards the massed flotilla of several hundred birds, bobbing up and down like pinkish-white boats in a yacht basin.

"Have you ever seen such a sight?" someone remarked as the skipper cut the motor, fearing

The greater flamingo showing their striking flight markings.

we would get caught in the reedy undergrowth.

"They're all pointing in the same direction," someone else added.

And so they were as if a mysterious signal controlled their actions.

"They aren't as pink as I thought they would be," someone else interjected.

Ben explained that these were the *greater* flamingos whose plummage was washed with pink and had outer wings tipped in a bright reddish-coral. The lesser flamingo was the one which was bright pink.

Suddenly, to keep us out of shallow water, the Njemps captain started the motor and by the hundreds, honking like geese, they rose in a wave showing their stunning black flight feathers.

They settled about a hundred yards away and again we maneuvered towards them.

I could have watched them feeding, head upside down, busy filtering food with their beaks, funny pink stilt-legs upheld, for hours. But they weren't keen on human peeping toms. So somehow the leader signaled to the huge group. A pinkish cloud moved in formation to a spot *across* the lake.

A tip: even my 300 mm telephoto lens wasn't powerful enough to hone in on a single bird. So bring a longer lens if you want a fine shot of flamingos. Also, use a polarizing filter to reduce the glare off the water.

"EVERYBODY READY FOR LEAKEY'S SNAKE FARM?" Ben asked gleefully.

I nodded, never having been to such a place I didn't know what to expect. Perhaps it was a spot where treacherous snakes swarmed and squiggled in a large pit—*a la* shades of the old movies.

It was located near the boat dock, and unknowingly we had passed it on the way in from the landing strip. Hesitantly we walked up to one of the many 8 foot tall wire enclosures which house all types of snakes from cobras to green mambas, one of Africa's most deadly snakes, with William, the jovial African snake handler. But we couldn't see a thing moving inside the grassy pens. Not a snake was in sight. William explained that they hide, usually curling up in a shady corner. I wondered why they didn't crawl up the sides of the enclosure and up over the top. But he said they just didn't and on some of the pens a wire screening was put across the top just in case.

Then William asked, "Would you like to see a green mamba?" And before we could say yes or no, he plunged a long steel pole inside, hauling out a hissing green bolt of lightning. Some of us scattered. But he conjoled us back, explaining that he knew how to hold the snake so we wouldn't get bitten.

"Do you want to see how I milk the venom?" he asked.

"No!" someone shot back.

"Yes!" another answered just as emphatically.

William smiled. Obviously he liked his job. Then he pulled back the roof of the mamba's mouth exposing the deadly fangs dripping a milky-like substance which would be used to produce an anti-venom serum.

Ben looked disgusted, so I asked why. "Oh," he said, "there are many mambas in Luoland, where I come from, and I hate and fear them as they are one of the few snakes which will aggressively come after you. They've killed many

Here's how to hold a deadly snake.

Calmly, William milks the venom from one of Africa's deadly snakes.

children."

Soon we were joined by mild-mannered Jonathan Leakey, one of the sons of Mary and Louis Leakey who did not follow in his parents anthropology footsteps. Like any good host, he wanted to show us the white-washed lab where the venom is stored. As we rounded the corner of the building, we bumped into pink-eyed, pink-eared rather rotund Susie.

Now Susie is Jonathan's three-year-old pet hippo who he adopted at one month of age when the mother was killed.

Susie waddled over to Jonathan and he affectionately gave her a pat.

"Isn't she adorable?" someone gushed.

"How do you keep her?" I asked inquisitively.

"We used to keep her in the house. She'd sit on the chairs or sofa, but now she's too big, and recently she's acquired a peculiar odor—it's similar to that of a skunk." Jonathan answered matter-of-factly. "So we've had to restrict her to the swimming pool where she spends most of her day anyway."

"What are you going to do with her when she gets full grown?" someone else asked, possibly knowing that hippos can weigh up to 4 tons at maturity.

"I plan on returning her back to the wild. Very soon, in fact." Jonathan said as Susie, perhaps knowing we were discussing her fate grunted and turned to leave, dejectedly ascending the steps to the pool, broad hips swaying.

I was sorry to see her go and gave her a slight pat as she went by.

(Note: as of this writing I've been told, Susie now lives in the lake and whenever she hears Jonathan's voice she paddles in for a pat.)

After we had bid William and Jonathan good-bye, thanking both of them, Ben asked, "That wasn't *so* bad, was it?"

All agreed that this was a worthwhile excursion.

Three-year-old Susie, the hippo, leaves to spend the afternoon in the swimming pool.

Susie receives a love pat from her master, Jonathan Leakey.

7 / Mara Masai — A Garden of Eden

FOR US, THE GARDEN OF EDEN of game reserves was Mara, an area of some 700 square miles, an extension of Tanzania's Serengeti National Park. Here, as perhaps it was in the beginning of time, there's a superabundance of game—large numbers of predators like the lion live alongside herds upon herds of various game animals. (Note: the largest concentration of lions in Kenya is located in Mara.)

Our 1:15 P.M. flight took us first to Nakura for refueling, thus giving us a chance to see the flocks of flamingos on the lake which the pilot noted weren't large now due to the migration, followed by an additional 40 minutes to reach Mara. From the air, Mara looked like an uncut green golf fairway without sand traps, only a few bent acacia trees here and there breaking the endless landscape.

Everyone was excited and slightly in awe of the enormity of grass, grass and more grass stretching before us. Here was an Africa totally unlike anything we had seen so far. (Note: the combined total of grassy savannah making up Mara and the Serengeti is bigger than Connecticut and Rhode Island put together.)

When we landed on the soft turf, Ben remarked off-handedly, "Usually we have to dive bomb to clear the animals off the runway. Every once and a while someone doesn't understand and thinks we are going to crash. It's great fun!"

I remembered how we wondered what the pilot was doing only a few hours ago when he did a Battle of Britain descent at Baringo. He had to clear the goats off the runway before picking us up. I would have liked to have been in on the chase.

Fred, reading my mind, gave me a wink,

Mara is big—on animals and space.

knowing I have a Red Baron mentality.

Although many stay at luxurious Keekorok or Serena Lodge in this reserve, our accomodations for the last two nights on safari were at Governors' Camp, a much older (15 years plus in operation) tented facility than Island Camp, again set on a concrete slab with its own shower and flush toilet (not everyone at Island Camp had a flush toilet, we had a chemical one which was fine).

Governors' provided us with gourmet cuisine —free wine served with five-course meals, even lunch—intimacy as there was room for only 30 people, some of whom were the titled heads of Europe this camp is so reknown, and a chance to be almost alone when viewing the animals.

OUR WINDING DOWN at Baringo made us eager and ready to go on the 4 P.M. game drive. The first animal spotted just outside the camp area, standing and grazing, their short tails constantly flickering from side to side like a metronome set on the fastest tempo, were Thomson's gazelles, called "Tommies" for short. Smaller, about two feet high, than the Grant's gazelle, and distinguished by the very black lateral stripe on the golden russet body, these animals usually become favorites of most everyone on safari. And they have an adorable way of seemingly bouncing along as if they were pogo sticks—head and tail erect and all four legs stiffly rigid—when alarmed. To see a plains come alive with these diminuative jumping gazelles is

The Tommy on the left is almost ready to bounce away. Notice the tail motion.

something I'll never forget.

"Darn," someone said disgustedly, "they won't stand still. I can't get a shot of them."

And it's true. You have to almost sneak up on them with your telephoto.

Not too many minutes later, a lioness reared her head out of the long grass. Since you don't have to stay on the roads in this reserve, we zipped over to the fallen acacia limb she seemed to be hiding under.

"Is she hurt?" someone asked.

"It doesn't appear so."

We maneuvered closer but she gave us a mean stare, her cold amber eyes seemingly telling us to stay back. We wondered why. Little did we know that a solitary female away from the pride indicates the birth of cubs. (Upon revisiting her a day and a half later, we discovered the cubs.)

"Stay back!" this lioness seems to say.

A lioness with newborn cubs nearby paces a fallen limb.

An angry lioness faces us.

Growling, she quickly got up, shook her tawny body, and then nervously proceeded to pace back and forth on the limb that had fallen from the adjacent hollowed out acacia tree.

For a moment, she stared past us into space, perhaps hoping for help to come. Then, curved tail twitching wickedly, she dropped off the log, and circled the old tree to face us.

Clearly we were *personas non gratis.*

We watched as she paused making up her mind whether to come at us or to stay close to the hollowed out acacia.

She advanced—and we moved.

Something ran down my cheek. It was a drop of rain. We were so engrossed in the lioness that we hadn't noticed it had clouded over. A light drizzle was falling. Fitting, I thought, for the mixed emotions we were feeling about her.

Note: with the start of the rainy season, the herds migrate, and so do the tourists—away from coming to East Africa. Mainly it rains in the late afternoon and evening, while during the day it is usually sunny. However, a grassy reserve like Mara can get quite soggy and difficult to navigate as the water was half-way up the wheels of our Land Rover. (We were there the first week in March.) But the animals enjoy the rain and are more active during this season.

IN FRONT OF A ROARING FIRE in the three-sided wood shelter used as a bar, we asked Ben about the closed border between Kenya and Tanzania, seven miles to the south. Shaking his head, he said thoughtfully, "There are two sides to the story. Tanzania says it closed the border because most of the tourist business came through Kenya with Tanzania only getting a few days revenue. It was as if the Serengeti was Kenya's not Tanzania's. But that's not really true. The tourists come to Kenya because our facilities are far better, and so is our attitude. We are pro-West and Tanzania isn't. Too, Tanzania's drivers and guides have always caused a hassle for me—they are like mad-men."

"We had been feeling badly," I said, "that we weren't able to see the Ngorongoro Crater and the Serengeti. But I began to change my mind when I heard that all Kenyan vehicles, even a brand-new Flying Doctor's plane, was confiscated by Tanzania when the border was closed a few weeks ago. The drivers, pilot and even some tourists were forced to walk back to Kenya. So I wasn't interested in being involved in that."

"Who knows what will happen next," Ben answered, giving me a pat on the arm. "Save something for your next visit. It will make you want to come back."

REVEILLE came at 5:30 A.M. with the jangle of coffee cups being set on the table in front of the tent. It was still pitch black outside. Fred lit the gas lantern to shave by its light. Gingerly, I unzipped the front flap, poking my head out to survey a verandah covered with puddles of water from the all-night rain. I brought in the tray containing the steaming black coffee and the slightly damp ginger snaps. It was cool. We dressed quickly. The game run was scheduled for slightly before 6:30 A.M. We were to come back for an outdoor safari barbecue breakfast at 9 A.M.

Sunrise comes while some of the animals still sleep.

An early morning expectancy hung over the savannah—and the group. The scene around the Land Rover was one of sleeping animals, some lying contentedly in the tall grass, and of a dim endless horizon, the sun beginning to poke its nose over it.

Almost immediately we were rewarded by what could have been a big boulder with hair in the grass. A lone sleeping lion. The Land Rover stopped within twenty feet of a fine male specimen, about 4 or 5-years-old, if my guess was correct. Usually lions don't pay attention to vehicles, knowing perhaps that they are neither dangerous nor edible, but the sound of the wheels squishing through the wet grass must have awakened him. We watched as this happened: he raises a shaggy head off large padded paws. Slowly the eyelids open revealing sleep-clouded yellow eyes. He yawns prodigiously giving us a glimpse of two white bottom canines and a foot or so of baby pink throat. He takes his time sitting up, knowing he has the whole day—peaceable days—before him. He frowns, accentuating a whiskered face that I had lost my heart

The portrait of the king of the beasts . . .

He awakes . . .

yawns . . .

sits up . . .

and majestically surveys his kingdom.

to through my 300 mm lens. Alertly, he turns to face us. A cowlick of the titian mane stands straight up, almost comically. I wanted to give him a comb to finish his morning grooming, but I'm sure he wouldn't have appreciated my interest. He appeared to be the strong, silent type.

Here, I thought, is the regal splendor of the king of his own country. He has a specific *personality* that leaves its imprint on the observer. That may be quite incomprehensible for anyone who's not been to Africa but it happens. Someone has written that apart from preserving the wild animals for conservation and tourist revenues, humans need to commune with them to attain "spiritual maturity." For me, it was a spiritual communion with the ancient symbol Christianity has had throughout the centuries for Christ.

NEXT, we had the audacity to rouse a honeymooner couple, the Land Rover rolling to a stop about fifteen feet from them. They looked foolishly in love—the male gentle and devoted lying close to his unruffled and inscrutable mate. Both were a far cry from the angry mother of the previous day or today's leonine marvel.

Biologically, the female comes into a weeklong estrus (heat) at about three-years-old with her urine and anal gland developing a strong smell, thus attracting any males in the vicinity. For the week they spend together they are inseparable with the female seductively lolling in the grass, often with a paw thrown over her mate's body or gently carressing him with her tail; he will lick her very tenderly. Touching in simple companionship is all important. He will mate with her every 20 or 30 minutes for hours at

The female of the honeymooner couple calmly lies close to her mate.

He foolishly rubs his eyes.

a time.

But our couple wasn't interested in this when we observed them. It appeared he was too engrossed in trying to get the sleep out of his eyes!

BY THE TIME WE RETURNED FOR THE 9:00 A.M. BREAKFAST, my stomach was growling. Still, the animals were worth the gauntness. Usually I wasn't a lover of early morning game drives due to the frustration a photographer feels about the 6:30 to 7:30 A.M. faint light which has little contrast for black and white and turns color shots to a murky blue. But all that changed this morning as we felt involved in the milieu of animal life—to see a zebra sleeping so soundly you presume it's dead until it bolts upright with fright or watch a lion rub its eyes like old Rip Van Winkle—well, it does something—humbles you—somehow.

Sooo good . . . breakfast safari style.

So the satisfying barbecue breakfast of sizzling bacon, sausage or ham, extra large eggs, toast, golden pancakes straight from the griddle, cereal and fresh fruits, set on round tables with canvas chairs in a grassy glade, was especially welcome.

We wanted to relax over hot tea, but Ben admonished, "If anyone wants to go back to the tent, do so now. We'll be leaving on another game drive in 10 minutes."

Although the safari way of life rotates between dining and game drives, we were never bored and the exhilaration or "high" from the animals causes energy to be burned up so I, a proverbial dieter, could eat as much as I wanted and never gain.

"WE'D LIKE TO SEE MORE LIONS," someone said enthusiastically to the driver.

"O.K. *bwana.* We see lions. Many lions. I take you!" The burly but friendly driver wheeled the Land Rover into a part of the reserve we hadn't explored during the morning's run.

"Look at that topi playing king-of-the-mountain on that rise," I said pointing to a 300 pound powerful antelope distinguished by a mask-like black blaze down the face, a glistening bluish-purple coat and ridged lyre-shaped horns. "He's a sentinel," Ben said. "Notice how they are stationed outside the main body of the herd."

"Why, yes," I answered, "there's one at 12, 2, 4—at two hour intervals—all around the perimeter. I wonder if anyone has done a study on them."

"I don't know about that," Ben said, "but they have such a good system that the herds flourish. Rarely does a lion get one of them."

Like the changing of the Queen's Dragoons, we watched as our sentry, giving us a nervous look, relinquished his post to another who had come up from the rear. How did they know

A topi sentry takes his job seriously.

when to relieve one another? Who posted the watch schedule? It was uncanny.

(Note: the Topi can be seen only in Mara in Kenya but is distributed throughout Tanzania and Uganda too.)

Also: we did not see one wildebeest on safari, I don't know why, but perhaps it was due to the state of their migration which begins in Tanzania. Too, some guidebooks describe armies of animals, ten abreast advancing across Mara or the Serengeti. Many years ago I imagine this was true but don't expect that now. Large herds—very large herds—*do* exist, so I was satisfied with this.

"A PRIDE," someone almost shouted. "See, over there lying in the long grass."

So it is. A large one. We begin to count—22 to be exact, all females, some old, some young, no small cubs, and all looking rather dopy as if they had too much Valium. One yawns indifferently. The other members barely stir. We wait, feeling slightly miffed—they aren't doing anything. We wait some more. I try to get a

A large pride lies indifferently in the grass. Notice the yawn.

group photo of all 22, but don't succeed.

"Wonder where papa is?" someone exclaimed. "A male with a harem like this must be really something."

But he's no where to be seen. It is known that males will chauvinistically go off alone or in the company of a friend in order to get away from the bickering of the females or the playfulness of the cubs. Still, they usually don't stray that far, staying close enough to keep an eye on things.

A female stands up. Perhaps she is the one with the most seniority, as a pride has a definite hierarchy. On top is a male or two males who may have teamed up, followed by the females in order of importance; the cubs come last, even when eating.

She pads slowly over to a termite hill, climbs to the top to stare out. Is she wondering when he is coming home? Or is she thinking about an upcoming kill?

More likely the latter.

"We go see more lions," the driver said impatiently, turning to the group.

"How about one with a real black mane?" someone requested.

Note: some believe that a black-maned lion is more viral and mature, but that's a myth. The mane varies from lion to lion in size and color ranging from a deep gold to black.

"Me find for you," he replied gleefully.

During that morning we saw 33 lions, and the total count over the two-day visit reached 50. There were lions in every conceivable state—covered with flies, squinting into the sun, sitting on their haunches, striding vigorously through the grass and dragging a kill back to the pride. (The only kill we actually were in on, and then we couldn't see it happen, was the one with the cheetahs in Samburu.)

A termite hill is a perfect lookout spot for a lioness.

A lion plagued by flies. Note: Elsa the lioness died from a parasite infection because she was in a weakened condition from fly bites.

The driver was proud of himself. He had done a fantastic job. "You happy now?" he asked.

How could we not be.

WE WERE SURPRISED when the driver, instead of returning for lunch, headed in still another direction. "Cheetahs," he said excitedly, "I know where."

We looked at one another as if to say this guy is too much for words.

Elegantly stretched out, taking a noon siesta was a family of four—mother and three almost fully-grown cubs. (Note: cheetahs don't form prides but family groups which stay together until the members are old enough to be on their own.)

Viewing them was an entirely different experience: instead of the pride's indolence, there was a sense of aristocratic dignity; their coats with a reddish-brown cast shone luxuriously in the sun radiating beauty and grace; their faces were unforgettable with expressions ranging from cat-like ferocity to a Parisian model's cold hauteur.

And they affect your nervous system—your heart thumps, your hands sweat—you are in awe, in much the same way a beautiful symphony, a sleek sports car, a fine race horse or a graceful athlete (or whatever) can "turn you on."

A cheetah has a sense of *presence.*

Too, their mien is one of status. Pharoahs had them in their courts as far back as 1500 B.C.; so did the Romans, and Louis XI of France owned and hunted with them (they are easily tamed as Joy Adamson's books *Spotted Sphinx* and *Pippa's Challenge* attest to). They are the Rolls Royces of a by-gone era.

Look at the expression on this face . . . it ranges from pugnaciousness . . .

. . . to benign imperturbability as a few flies alight on his nose

. . . to enigmatically serene grandeur.

So we were especially grateful to our Masai driver for ushering us into the court of "the prince of beasts."

LUNCH consisted of an on-the-house glass of red or white wine, an excellent pawn cocktail, hot creamy celery soup, tender moussaka, fresh peas, and a sideboard laden-down with fresh fruit pies.

The repast and the morning's animal marvels were beyond our wildest dreams, so we weren't too upset when the 4 P.M. game drive was rained out. Yet, when 5 P.M. arrived and the downpour had diminished to a drizzle, we asked Ben, "How about it? Will our driver take us out again?"

Is it love? Take a look at the knobby knees too.

Again we set out under gunmetal skies. Our driver throwing caution to the wind laughed uproariously each time the Land Rover almost bogged down in the mud. I had visions of being initiated into a *walking* safari in the not too distant future.

But the effort was worth it. At what was the farthest point away from camp, we caught sight of two Masai giraffes, whose intricate star and leaf markings clearly distinguish them from the patchwork reticulated sub-species seen in Meru and Samburu.

They were "necking," long necks swinging back and forth. Although giraffes fight by necking, it appeared that these two weren't taking it seriously, as they nuzzled each other, swaying like long stem roses.

These bulls, many which weigh 3000 pounds emit a subtle power—a well-placed hoof can decapitate a lion as well as a resiliency, shown by the fact a 150 pound new-born sustains a 5-foot drop as it comes into the world, since the giraffe gives birth in the upright position. Imagine how the human population would decrease if we followed suit. Yet, they are gentle creatures too, going about their business of feeding on the whistling-thorn acacia (their long, hairy lips protect them from the spike-like thorns) and eating up to 75 pounds of this watery vegetation every 24 hours.

And to watch them walk 14 feet or more above the ground with a haughty expression, immense 6-foot legs swinging forward, mane rippling across a taffy-colored back, is thrilling. But they don't stay around for that long, melting quickly into the acacia woodland.

Ben explained that man has poached the giraffe because he finds his meat tasty, the tail useful for fly whisks and the hide strong for sandals.

(For lighthearted, good reading about these animals, obtain *Raising Daisy Rothschild,* by Betty & Jock Leslie-Melville.)

A giraffe can run at 35 miles an hour.

THE RAIN HAD STOPPED. An eerie silence had fallen over the plains. It was dinnertime for the predators. As the sun, low on the horizon haphazardly touched the savannah with light, we could make a dark menacing form fleeing across the grassland after an unknown shape.

Suddenly, the lead vehicle exploded in hot pursuit, honking its horn loudly.

"What's going on?" Fred asked excitedly.

"I don't know," Ben answered, poking his head out of the window. "Let's find out."

Soon we saw, about 100 yards in front of us, a "Tommy," who literally flies across the ground, fleeing from a spotted hyena.

I can't stand it," someone said, putting up an arm to shield their eyes, "I don't want to look."

"I don't blame you," someone else added, "the hyena is the worst of all the predators. It grabs ahold of the animal's back and begins to

Like a camel, the giraffe can go for long periods without liquid as its food is 74% water. Also, it's not known to bathe.

The bad guy of the plains—the hyena.

eat its prey alive. At least the other predators like the lion or cheetah kills its victim first."

For many, the hyena with its very low sloping, almost slinky back, drab spotted body and powerful jaws set in an ugly sneering face is the epitome of a bad actor. And perhaps he is. But looks can be deceiving as the observations of Jane and Hugo van Lawick-Goodall indicate in their book, *Innocent Killers* (try and obtain a copy of this—it's good). They note that even though the hyena eats its prey alive, the victim is dead in several minutes, and usually doesn't feel the pain as they are in a state of severe shock. While the lion who has a reputation of being a "clean killer," may take as long as 10 minutes to suffocate its quarry.

So who's to say which is the worst way to die?

Too, the hyena has been praised for its thrifty use of all the carcass—everything that can be is eaten, the bones are crushed for the marrow and the last drop of blood is licked clean from the grass; even the mane or tail, rolled up in a ball, may be brought back to the den as a plaything for the cubs. So—

Still, there's a happy ending to this story. The lead vehicle, after jarring the silence for what seemed like an interminable length of time pulled up alongside our Land Rover. Breathlessly they explained, "We saved him! We saved him! He was almost down and the hyena had started on his tail. But we rattled him so much that he had to let go, and then the Tommy got away!"

So if you ever see a Tommy without a tail, perhaps it's the one saved by our group whose faces were shining in triumph.

And everyone received a dividend for this good deed—the African sun set off a Fourth-of-July display.

THE LAST DAY ON SAFARI DAWNED. I felt sad. Yet, there would be little time for emotion what with a schedule of 2 game drives, a visit to the Masai who own the lands of Mara, and a stop at the hippo pool, before flying to Nairobi to repack our luggage at the New Stanley, attend a farewell dinner party, and catch an after midnight flight to London.

A tip: almost too much is crammed into the last day. So try and space it out by staying overnight (that's an extra) in Nairobi or if you do go on to London spend a few rest days there. Too, you might want to investigate the direct flight to New York that makes several stops along the way but at least you don't have to change planes. It leaves several times a week.

By now we were seasoned "safariers," capable of identifying a whole range of previously unfamiliar mammals and birds, so the morning's game drive was like putting on an old shoe, familiar, comfortable and enjoyable.

Again the drama of the hunters and the hunted became a stark reality. In the early blue morning light, we saw yesterday's slumbering cheetah family was on the hunt.

Now we could distinguish mother from her three teenagers by the shaggy ruff at the back of their necks. They were nearly her size but lacked her haughty dignity.

Like a school mistress, mother appeared to be putting her young through the workbook exercise of hunting as cheetahs must be taught to kill.

First, they walked in an unhurried unison—deliberate and sedate, without being the least bit menacing. Then they would periodically stop to stare off into the distance.

Mother would twist her regal head back to look at what, we didn't know, and not once did she or the cubs acknowledge we were even there. This gave us a funny feeling as if the cheetah lived in a world unto itself—proud, yet not prideful.

Again she would proceed, stopping here and there to carry out the same ritual, cubs following suit. Soon they came upon an uprooted acacia, which each animal climbed to sharpen its claws, lithely jumping down.

Gone was the tension we felt while watching the Samburu cheetahs. This mother gave the impression she had all the time in the world for making a kill. Yet, she didn't fool us as we knew

Mother and her almost two-year-old adolescents—watching on a hunt.

The cheetah displays an almost aquiline beauty.

Like any cat, a cheetah likes to sharpen its claws.

underneath that placid exterior was a tightly wound up body capable of feats equal to Nureyev's leaps and Julius Erving's basketball dunks, all which defy description.

From time to time, the cubs lacking her intense concentration would flop down in the grass to rest. But she wasn't about to give in to them. On she went with this stop and go behavior pattern, as if to teach them diligence. Or maybe she knew that a meal might be waiting ahead in the long grass.

Almost simultaneously, Fred and I ran out of film. I smiled. It always seemed to happen when we least expected it.

Then the driver turned to us and said, "She won't catch anything if we follow. It's not good to stay."

I didn't know that cheetahs need "elbow room" to hunt, and that it was very likely that she and her cubs would go hungry if we didn't leave them alone.

Although we understood, I wished we could have followed, perhaps forever, she was so mesmerizing. In fact, I felt bewitched.

Lacking a rigid backbone, when a cheetah is in motion, it's like a spring, coiling and uncoiling.

A male walks determinedly back to the pride . . .

. . . knowing perhaps that his lioness has brought home the bacon—a warthog—for breakfast.

So, we turned around, heading south towards camp, and were rewarded by a lioness dragging a dull grey 150 pound warthog back to the pride. Almost immediately to the left, quickly striding through the blue-green grass, appeared her lord and master, as if he had been called to breakfast.

It is known that a lion eats approximately 20-30 pounds of meat a day—which isn't that much—totaling about 10-20 antelopes per year.

Next, we chanced upon another honeymooner pair, but this time she was hopelessly in love, head docilely resting on her forepaws, while he, virle and looking like the Charles Atlas of lions, was vigilant and clear-witted. He looked in the prime of life, measuring about 8-9 feet from the nose to the tip of the tail and perhaps weighing close to 350 pounds. When he rippled his powerful muscles ominously, we became edgy, knowing that a lion with one swat can knock down a 400 pound animal. We moved on. Note: the color photograph on the cover and in the back section is of this lion.

Look at our tire tracks. We were almost on top of this pair.

Lastly, when the lead vehicle stopped to pay its last respects to the angry lioness of the initial game drive in Mara, they discovered three helpless funny looking cubs in the hollowed-out acacia; mother was nowhere to be seen, at that moment, at least.

A newborn cub is blue-eyed, measures about 12 inches, seems to be all head and feet with a tail that's more stumpy than anything else, has a thick coat and may be spotted. But they grow rapidly, multiplying their birth weight of two pounds almost 200 times by the time they reach maturity.

Suddenly, before we attempted to circle the acacia to peer in too, mother appeared, snarling, tail lashing. Since we had visions of her jumping on top of the Land Rover and clawing someone, we stopped dead in our tracks. She wasn't about to allow anyone a tire step closer.

We—intimidated—and rightly so, decided it was time for breakfast.

It was impossible to get close to a group of newborn cubs.

BEN, TOTALLY OUT OF CHARACTER, seemed to be dawdling over breakfast. And I wondered why. Perhaps the long hours of playing housemother to the ten of us had finally taken its toll, although he had previously mentioned we were one of his best groups. Then, snapping out of his languor, he said, "All right, everyone ready. We'll make a five minute stop at the Masai village before going to the hippo pool."

"Why only five minutes?" I asked hesitantly.

"You'll see when we get there," he answered —giving me a wink, straight white teeth gleaming. His good humor had returned.

O.K., I thought, if there's something to buy I can do it in a short period of time. Someone in Group B had purchased a red, white, brown and black Masai shield that I felt would be stunning on a wall.

A word about the Masai: of the 150,000 in Kenya, all are very tall, lean, individuals who for years have been nomadic cattlemen wandering the plains in search of good grazing lands for their white hump-backed livestock. They believe they rightfully own all the world's cattle, although I don't know why, and like the Lake Baringo Njemps, a man's wealth is measured by the size of his herd. But their fame has come from a fierce reputation as warriors. Even the lion is afraid of them, as they used to have a ritual of spearing a lion and drinking his blood. (Lions have transmitted this fear down through the generations, thus giving a Masai on foot a wide berth.) And too, they are known as the tribe which still drinks the blood of their cattle.

Climbing out of the Land Rover, the villagers decked out in spears, rows and rows of colorful beads, elaborate headdresses and long earrings, started towards us. As they advanced, so did a black swarm of nasty flies. I felt as if a dark buzzing cloud had suddenly blotted out the sun. They were everywhere—on my head, nose, arms—I could almost taste them.

But the Masai seemed puzzled by our discomfort as they nonchalantly posed for photographs (5 shillings a person, even the child), the faces of the round-faced babies crawling with insects.

Lions fear the courageous Masai.

In less than five minutes, we were back in the Land Rover urging the driver to go faster and faster in hopes of blowing out the remaining bugs.

"See," said Ben laughingly, "I knew we wouldn't stay long. There are always flies in the village as the Masai make their houses out of cow manure. But I have a great respect for them. They are a tough people."

By the time we reached the Mara River which flows westward into Lake Victoria and its hippo pool, all our winged friends had scattered. I couldn't quite imagine what a hippo pool would be like (I knew of an office pool and a swimming pool but—) until we reached the steep riverbank and looked down into a ringed group of 33 hippos submerged in a slow-moving part (pool) of the river. Their enormous heads set with periscope eyes, slit-like nostrils and short ears were visible every three to five minutes as they surfaced blowing water noisily from their nostrils as they took a breath. Bobbing up and down they looked like a group of wet-suited scuba divers learning how to clear their face masks.

The Masai women shave their heads and wear beautiful beadwork. Notice the flies on the baby.

Hippos form a useful function of grazing at night on riverside vegetation, thereby keeping streams from clogging up.

The Greek name for hippo is "River Horse." Look at those beady eyes.

They watched us warily, the sun glinting off burnt copper backs, but on the whole, none of them had the charm and personality of "Susie."

A NOISY CHATTER FILLED the dining room during the last stupendous lunch, and I noticed how adaptable and knowledgeable everyone had become. We had grown-up, a wee bit more, if that's possible with increasing age, as the over two-week safari drama had stretched us. But isn't Africa supposed to do this?

I felt as guests in this peaceable kingdom, we were uninvited by the animals but somehow they tolerated us and even seemed to know we were necessary if they were to be preserved.

Then I began to ruminate on how lion fossils discovered in European Stone Age caves attested to the fact they did roam throughout that continent but now are extinct. The same is true in North Africa where Assyrian kings hunted lions from their chariots; their range extended through the Middle East and India too. But now only Africa lays claim to a large lion population. And the same story can be told about the cheetah, while the leopard seemed already extinct to me, even here in Africa.

But the question I couldn't get out of my mind was: will the Masai tribesmen we saw today conserve all this?

Naturally, I didn't know the answer, although I've been told that the Masai and most Africans are conservative people.

So when the plane taxied off the waving grass runway heading north for Nairobi and home for us, I said a silent prayer that this Garden of Eden wouldn't be turned into two-story condominiums and golf courses with difficult bunkers.

How To Plan a Safari and What To Do in Nairobi

PLANNING YOUR TRIP — The first step is to chose a tour. I discovered safaris come in a wide range, including travel by lazy camel, horse, balloon, chartered plane, foot or zebra-striped minibus.

Also, safaris come in three price ranges. The least expensive are the minibus or road packages offered through various tour operators (Lindblad Travel, Abercrombie & Kent, Nilestar, Caravan, General Tours, Park East, Maupintour, Percival, Four Winds, Hemphill Harris, Thorn Tree, Cheetah Safaris, World Adventure, Unitours, African Explorers, Travcoa, Questers, Esplanade (U.S. agents for England's Swan Ltd.),Raymond & Whitcomb, Brien Merriman, WEXAS, East African Travel and many more—please don't be upset if yours isn't mentioned, they all are good; see your travel agent for specifics) in conjunction with various airlines (Pan Am, British Airways, KLM, Sabena, Alitalia and others). These last 15-16 days and aren't anymore expensive than a cruise or a stay at a good resort (since prices, like airfares, change often, they won't be quoted; see your travel agent). Next, is the "wing" safari which we chose; it's less strenuous than the road trips and more extensive in that you have more actual hours of game viewing, and at times visit more remote areas of Kenya. And lastly, the most expensive "tented" safari is very popular as they set up camp right where the animals are located (a combination of tents and wings is offered by some tour operators). Too, you can make up your own safari, the cost really isn't that much more. Also, there are packages available with many stops in Africa, one of them being Kenya. Another option: obtain 1-9 day packages directly in Nairobi.

A tip: if you can afford the time and the extra airfare, think about breaking up your flight to Africa into segments—a few days in an European city, or better yet, spend time in Nairobi at the beginning or the end of your trip. Another option: you'll pick up extra time by flying direct from New York to Nairobi.

WHEN TO COME — What's the best time of the year to go? Anytime—spring, summer, winter, fall. We wanted a winter vacation and we knew it would be warm in Kenya as the equator cuts right across it, so we chose February only to find the seasons reversed—it was August, weather-wise in Kenya. That was perfect, however, as the winter months are the most popular due to the 80-90 degree Caribbean-like weather (but it can get as high as 114 degrees at Lake Baringo and 55 degrees at night in the Aberdares). Too, in February, there's a chance to see large numbers of young born into the herds. Then the rains come in March, April and May but even these shouldn't deter a trip as they arrive in the late afternoon and evening with the weather being just fine during the day.

Remember though, our summer months will be their coolest, due to the reverse in seasons, getting down to the 40's at night in the Aberdares while the days will be delightful at about 70 degrees. Also, another short rainy season occurs in late October-November. So, in short, it's possible to go to Kenya throughout the year.

WHAT TO TAKE — As far as clothes go, a safari outfit is a must (two works well, a long and a short sleeve; for women, one with a skirt to keep cool during the hotter months of December through March) if you want to get into the swing of things—and even if you don't, it's still a good investment.

A tip: there are scores of safari outfitters in Nairobi located in and around most of the hotels where you can buy low-cost safari jackets, slacks and skirts right off the

the rack or have them made up in a day's time (it's like buying clothes in Hong Kong in this respect). Recommended: the Hilton arcade shops, especially Yellow Bird, which sells a 100% polyester outfit that's lightweight and dries like a dream; it's not warm either. Also, Copra, near the New Stanley is good.

Another good reason to purchase an outfit in Nairobi is that their fabrics seem to be just the right weight for the African climate; also, note: the polyester and cotton outfits sold in the states are excellent too; so are the 100% cotton even though they need ironing to look good.

FOR NAIROBI — bring some good-looking city clothing, such as a pant-suit, dressy dress for dining out, a suit or sport coat (for men), and even one long skirt. Remember Nairobi is a British city. Wear your safari outfit during the day, if you like.

FOR THE BUSH — *the following list was made up for the warm safari months* of December through March, so if you are going at a different time, remember it will be much cooler. For example, bring long sleeve shirts, heavy sweaters and *wool* or heavy cotton slacks (jeans even) for the cooler months. Bring a lightweight rain coat to wear in Nairobi too.

- a hat (both men and women; a must to protect from sun and dust; I've noticed in some sport catalogs that pith helmets are trying to make a comeback— normally they aren't worn, but buy one if you like)
- a pair of boating, tennis or canvas shoes which you may want to give away after the safari due to the dust permeating every crack and crevice
- a pair of comfortable shoes for evening wear
- a sweater (in some areas like the Aberdares, a fire is lit at night to take the chill off; mornings are cool too)
- 2 or more pairs of slacks (normally these are part of your safari outfit but take at least one or two extra pairs for wear in the evening; preferable lightweight pairs, even seersucker; denim that's new in the very hot areas can be too heavy and warm)
- 4 different tops of shirts for day and evening (a blend of cotton for coolness and polyester for drying; as I said before—see the index—some lodges provide a laundry service if you stay two or more nights; but note: all laundry is done by hand and hung to dry outside as electric clothes dryers are unheard of in the bush, so if it rains, which it does in the Aberdares and Mara, your clothes come back wet. Still, the laundry is done beautifully—your tee-shirts are even returned to you ironed)
- a swim suit as most lodges have pools
- 1 or 2 skirts for women (some may want to get out of hot slacks and dress up in the evening; my safari outfit had a skirt which I wore all the time)
- a sundress (it did get warm!)
- socks for men and women too (a must to protect from chiggers; bring wool socks for cool months)
- pair of hiking shorts
- a lightweight bathrobe/slippers
- sunglasses
- personal toilet articles should include one can of insect repellent *as well as* a small can of insect killer like Raid for mosquitoes at night
- 2 pairs of pajamas/nightgowns (which is natural as is underwear)
- flashlight, another must
- suntan lotion, again a must
- a normal supply of medicine (diarrhea and problems with the water don't normally occur, unless you are overtired, as the country is very clean)
- an electric razor with a rechargable unit (sometimes there's no power)
- small items like soap, shampoo, pocket packs of Kleenex, wash 'n dries, washcloth, soap powder or liquid, fold-up plastic hangers, clothesline (travel type), extra pair of glasses or contacts, instant coffee, plastic drinking cup, travel alarm clock, binoculars, moisturizers, hand creams, and hair conditioners

But the best advice is to bring as little as possible (the above list isn't that much when you lay it out on a bed). Too, the hotels will safely store your city clothes for nominal charge when in the bush.

Also, the wing safari people are given a special suitcase that's quite roomy to use (the baggage isn't weighed so don't worry about the poundage) and they are allowed two pieces of hand luggage which is far plenty.

A tip: although soft luggage has become the rage these days, it might be wise to dust off your battered Samsonite and take it instead, as luggage has been slit open, and the contents removed at the airport.

Another tip about hairdressers: they are good in the hotels, but bring a wig for the bush, or have a permanent before you go. Blow-dry equipment usually will not work, especially if you are tenting.

HEALTH REQUIREMENTS — Start taking your malaria pills (chloroquine, see your doctor for a prescription) before you leave home (they must be started one week prior to arrival); the government's eradication measures have been successful and malaria is no longer a great hazard but still it's better to be safe than sorry.

Inoculations are needed for smallpox (most countries

don't require this anymore; valid for three years—on revaccination, my arm was swollen) and yellow fever (valid for 10 years). Note: these two are best given on the same day; usually the yellow fever is obtained at a public health facility.

Also, cholera is needed (valid for 6 months) and it's a good idea to have a tetanus booster or shots as one of the members of our group tore open the top of his head on a jagged edge in a Land Rover (nothing serious but it did bleed a lot).

These vaccinations are listed by your doctor (remember they must be certified too; ask where) on a yellow International Health Certificate obtained from your travel agent.

And against the chance of something really serious happening (appendicitis, heart attack), the wing safari costs include a $20 fee to the "Flying Doctors' Society of Africa," a wonderful group who has airlifted many patients out of the bush, thus saving their lives.

A word about the water: in Nairobi, it's perfectly safe—out of the tap and on the table. But in the bush, the table and carafe water are safe (not the tap), so purchase bottled water for brushing your teeth—it comes in very large bottles that last several days, and is readily available.

Lastly, a note about the most common occurrence acquired while traveling—diarrhea: it's unlikely you will get it as the water is safe (note the above) and so are the vegetables. We ate all the lettuce, tomatoes, cucumbers, etc., served to us without any problems.

WHAT ABOUT CAMERA EQUIPMENT & FILM — Most important is to bring enough film, as many end up paying almost double the cost per roll when they run out (film is terribly expensive in Africa). As photographers, my husband and I *each* shot approximately two rolls of 36's *per day*—total 55 rolls. I do the black and white using Tri-X and a red filter and he does color prints using Kodacolor II and a polarizing filter. If you are using slide film, I would get Kodachrome instead of Ektachrome because it has a yellow cast which is needed to bring up the yellows of Africa. My rule of thumb is to shoot blue film (higher ASA) if your subject will be mainly blue-green, otherwise stick with the Kodachrome. The only exception to this is on the early morning game drives when the light is *poor*—then use the faster Ektachrome 200 or the new Kodacolor 400.

So bring enough film, even if you aren't photographically minded (at least 20 rolls).

Also, do NOT have any film developed abroad or shipped home. Bring it back for developing (too, don't use those cheapy developers, as I've known more people whose film has been lost or damaged; use Kodak).

As far as camera equipment goes, I can't stress strongly enough—don't leave home without a telephoto lens—a 200 or 300 mm is a must; if you have a zoom—fine, but most of your shots will be at the longest focal length. (For me, the zoom is a hassle with poorer optics, so I use a 200 or 300 mm lens). For close-up bird shots obtain a 500-600 mm lens, otherwise you will be disappointed (I was). So beg, borrow or steal a telephoto and even if you don't know how to use it, someone in the group most likely will help you.

Other lenses to take: a normal 50 mm; a wide angle isn't necessary as it reduces the object size, something you don't want in Africa. I also use a 55 mm lens on one of our two Nikons for close-up shots of signs.

Take a flash only if you have room; there are only few spots where it will be useful such as the Bomas of Kenya, the Ark, and Samburu. Also, I didn't use a tripod or sand bags; learn how to hand-hold your camera.

Other camera tips are scattered throughout the text—see the index.

Also, take a pair of binoculars for spotting the animals—a must.

Note: the Africans can be photographed if they are paid (for us, prices ranged from 50 cents to $12 for a large group or tribe, the cost being split up among the tour members). But it's forbidden to photograph the President of Kenya.

Too, remember to register your camera equipment with the U.S. Customs Service before you leave home; if you don't you might have to pay duty on these items. At the customs office you'll need a bill of sale or an insurance policy which lists the items before they will issue the necessary document.

ABOUT CURRENCY — The unit of currency is the Kenyan shilling. At this writing, the exchange rate is about 8 shillings to the dollar. But the important thing to be aware of is that Kenya has a tight security control—this means that upon arrival at the airport you'll be given a Foreign Exchange Form which has to be filled out and *stamped* properly (if no stamp is available, ask for a receipt) each time you exchange money (this can be done at hotels or banks, hours 9 A.M. to 1 P.M. daily). This same form—with all your money accounted for—has to be turned in at the airport when you depart for home. (If you have an excess of Kenyan money at the end of your stay, you'll be able to change it back into dollars *as long as* you are able to produce a receipt showing the original exchange of dollars into shillings; without the receipt, forget it.) Remember to save some shillings (ask the tour guide for the correct amount) for the airport departure tax—it can't be paid in dollars.

Also note: the duty free shop at the airport *doesn't* accept Kenyan money for its items, so don't think those extra shillings can be used up there.

It's best to bring traveler's checks but note: out in the bush, it was hard to cash them at times, so get your shillings in Nairobi first.

How much money will be needed in the bush? Bring at least $250 *in Kenya shillings* for wine or liquor as these purchases must be paid for immediately (they can't be added to your room bill). Add an extra lump sum for those "must have" purchases in the lodge gift shops (note: credit cards were not honored everywhere either). Only in Nairobi were credit cards honored, but again not everywhere.

Remember to keep your money, passport, and other valuables locked up in the hotel's safety deposit box. If you don't want to carry much money with you into the bush, it's possible to use the hotel's box even when you are away (we did; just ask).

ABOUT PASSPORTS, VISAS AND THE AIRPORT — A valid passport is needed for entry into Kenya and so is a visa (obtained through your travel agent or by writing the Kenya Tourist Office, 15 East 51st Street, New York, N.Y. 10022; telephone, 212-486-1300. The Kenya Embassy in Washington, 2249 R Street also handles requests). Upon arrival at the airport, which is an old structure (not air-conditioned) but adequate, you'll need both. Clearing customs is quite easy, although at times you don't know which line to stand in. You'll be given the above mentioned currency exchange form and if you want to exchange money in the airport you can—the lines are usually long.

Taxis are easy to obtain but bargain for the price (we paid $8 for the 20-minute ride into Nairobi).

The only time the airport seems chaotic is upon departure when many flights are leaving at about the same time. Arrive early as there is a line to stand in to return your currency exchange form, an airport departure tax to be paid, (remember in Kenyan shillings) besides the normal baggage and flight check-in's.

A tip: keep a 3 x 5 index card in your wallet of your passport number (some people even recommend photocopying the title page in case of theft, as this copy can speed up the issuance of a new one), the number sequence on your traveler's checks, and other data of importance. You'd be surprised how much key information can be crammed onto this small card and slipped into a wallet.

ABOUT SECURITY — Don't be upset by the notices telling you to be worried about crime in East Africa. Yes, it's important to lock up your valuables even in New York City, for that matter, and to carry a minimum of money on the streets. And too, you will find people who will beg (I give because Jesus said, 'If you give unto the least of these, you've given unto Me,' but that's me—you do what you feel is best). And you don't have to be intimidated after dark from going to any restaurant or club, provided you take a taxi (ask at the hotel what the price should be and then establish it before you get in).

We walked all over town shopping for bargains (see the next section on Nairobi for shopping tips). And we discovered walking around the New Stanley, the Hilton, City Hall, etc.—downtown—is fine, no problems. But the walk between the University, across from the Norfolk, and the downtown is just okay—take a taxi.

But note: I don't want to lull you into complacency. Don't leave suitcases opened in the room and leave for dinner, let's say, as some items may be missing when you return (this happened to a friend). Never leave traveler's checks lying around (the most common trick is to remove center ones so you won't notice some are missing), and watch your camera equipment. Don't talk to street people who usually are con artists (many are teenagers). Still, by and large the African is a wonderful and friendly person, only a few spoil it for the rest.

OTHER SAFARI TIPS THAT MAY SAVE YOUR LIFE — Always carry a flashlight at night to scare away any wild animals; if there is a ranger on duty, have him walk you back to the room (someone was attacked by a buffalo who didn't). Remember, these are wild animals you are viewing so don't get out of the vehicles, and don't wander away from the lodges to take a closer picture, let's say of an elephant, as it might charge! Someone once offered an elephant food—he was killed.

What To Do in Nairobi

DINING IN NAIROBI — Try the truly gourmet Alan Bobbe's Bistro, billed as a corner of France in the heart of Africa, which it is! (It's about a three-minute taxi ride from the New Stanley, located at Caltex House, Koinage Street, phone: 21152; open for lunch and dinner, reservations required, credit cards accepted; dinner for 2 with wine, about $35, service added to bill, no tipping).

The "burger corner" at the Hilton is where we ate most of our lunches—it features such burger goodies as the Mt. Kenya with onions, tomato, and pickles or the Africana with chili sauce and bacon. Another good choice, we were told, is the Norfolk Hotel's Sunday brunch for less than $5. Friends also said that they had a delightful lunch at the revolving restaurant on the top of the Kenyatta Conference Center.

Also recommended: any of the hotel dining rooms like the Hilton's coffee shop and Grill Room or the New Stanley's "Carvey" buffet, served on Mondays only, in the ballroom where we sampled impala, gammon (a type of ham), pork, roast beef and lamb—outstanding.

Sorry to say, the New Stanley has made its Tate or Grill Room into a private club (The Bacchus), so dinner is out here, but it's possible to obtain a temporary membership by calling the Club Manager or writing ahead; note: the Club is heavily booked over the weekends.

For other restaurants, see the listings in Nairobi's *What's On* free guide.

As far as spirits go—the local beer, served in large bottles, is delicious—ask for Tuskers or Pilsner *baridi,* which means cold in Swahili (a very useful word to know, especially after a hot day in the bush). Note: many of the bars have been closed too and made into private clubs.

After dark, except for movies and restaurants Nairobi almost closes down. (People have been warned not to go out after dark, but we did without any trouble.) Yet, there is the Starlight Club opposite the Pan Afric Hotel, while the newest club is right in the New Stanley—The Bacchus, a discotheque, mentioned above, which stays open until 4 A.M.

TIPPING IN NAIROBI — This might be as good a place as any to mention it. At the airport (tour groups are transferred as a group so they won't have this), 2 shillings (about 50 cents) per suitcase; the same for hotel porters. Don't be upset if your bills (restaurant and hotel) are higher than the basic rate. Added on will be a 10% tax, a 2% training levy (it helps support the government tourism college) and a 10% service charge. So you will not tip if your check includes these extras; many spots mention this in the published rate. For bar bills 10% is normal.

For your driver, if he does a good job (ours always did), 35-40 shillings per day for the group in one car. Game rangers get 10 shillings per day.

At the end of the trip, your guide (like Ben) should get approximately $30 per person or $60 per couple. (Now you know why it's so important to bring at least $250 into the bush, what with tips, bar bills, costs for photographing the Africans, etc.).

SHOPPING IN NAIROBI — It's a delight to shop for jewelry, gems, masks, sculpture, batiks, baskets, crystal and handicrafts.

Shops open early, by 8:30 A.M. with closing around 4:30 or 5 P.M.; some stay open longer till 7 P.M. The majority of shops will be closed on Saturday afternoons, but we found some in the Hilton arcade that were open even on Sundays.

Try Studio Arts 68 Ltd., half a block from the New Stanley on Standard Street for those not too expensive gifts to take home like hand-blocked placemats, aprons, children's toys, baskets, and just about everything (note: we weren't able to bargain here), farther down Standard in the Phoenix Arcade, opposite the 680 Hotel is Cottage Crafts Gallery, sponsored by the National Christian Council of Kenya, which has lovely handicrafts, at reasonable prices.

For not too expensive masks and carvings of giraffes, elephants, etc., take a walk down Kenyatta Avenue to African Heritage Ltd. (they also maintain a smaller shop in the Samburu Lodge, where credit cards were not accepted, so take traveler's checks). If you are willing to pay the price for some truly outstanding carvings of African heads, masks, buffalo herds, or other art like batiks and oil paintings by up and coming artists, then visit Kumbu Kumbu, in the Hilton arcade, or Watatu Gallery, upstairs off Standard Street. (We purchased 3 unique pieces at the Africa Cultural Gallery, near the corner of Kaunda & Kimathi Streets, but all arrived broken. Tip: carry your purchases home.)

A tip: the masks and other carved objects sold by the local street vendors can be bargained for at good prices.

It's hard to believe this is a lifesize sculpture of a tribesman.

A scary but interesting carved mask.

Out in the bush, prices may be lower but the selection can be limited and often the shop hours don't jive with the tours, so shop in Nairobi, it's more fun.

If you are after jewelry, every shop seems to carry it; we bargained for a celtic cross at The Village on Kimathi Street. For gems, the African Jewels Ltd. in International House, near the Hilton, sells Tsavorite, the new gemstone discovered by Tiffany's president, as well as malachite and other minerals (prices are high but so is the quality).

Since I'm a lover of crystal, I was delighted with Rowland Ward on Standard Street, whose glassware with animal engravings is as beautiful as a Steuben (expensive but selling for double the price in New York; credit cards accepted).

Also, don't overlook a visit to the famous Maridadi fabrics factory or stop into their shop on Tom Mboya Street, opposite Gill House. If you are afraid the prints will be wild, don't be, as they are like the Lily fabrics of Florida. Take a look at something right off the rack at any of the shops in the Hilton arcade too (I purchased a gorgeous long hand-screened wrap-around for under $20).

Too, many will want to visit the East African Wildlife Society's showroom, featuring a gift shop of wildlife cards, prints, paintings, and even children's toys, on the mezzanine floor off the Hilton arcade; we were so pleased with our visit that we became members.

For safari outfit shopping, see the section under *What To Take* for specific store recommendations.

Note: not long ago, the Kenya government banned all big-game hunting. This was followed by an order to shut down all stores selling animal trophies (hides) and curios (ivory items). This is a wonderful effort to stop the poaching of the animals. But personally I wonder if this still will go on because European cities like Paris or Munich sell leopard skin coats (they have been banned in America; ivory hasn't been banned here yet but it's under consideration). So the banning has to world-wide to be effective.

PLACES OF INTEREST IN NAIROBI — The most important places are: the Nairobi National Park (the best time to visit is in the P.M.); the National Museum (with the new Leakey Wing); the Snake Park; and the Bomas of Kenya, a government-run cultural center, featuring recreated villages in a park-like setting (sort-of like an African Williamsburg), and in the main building, a dance group made up of members from Kenya's major tribes who perform authentic tribal dances. Arrive early (cost $3 adults; $1.50 children) to walk through the models of the villages or take the guided tour after the dancing.

If you are pressed for time, it's possible to do all four attractions by hiring a car and driver (prices vary all the way up to $45, depending on the places you are visiting) in a six-hour span, by beginning at noon, as distances are short.

A tip: you can arrange for a car and driver or a rent-a-car (driving is on the left, British style and traffic is heavy at peak hours) through your travel agent in the U.S.

There's a revolving restaurant on top of the tall Kenyatta Conference Center.

OTHER PLACES TO VISIT — Stroll through the modern and flower-filled Nairobi University. I'm sure you will be impressed as we were. Perhaps combine your visit, as we did with a "look see" at the Norfolk Hotel (directly across the street)—their courtyard aviary is outstanding.

Take a walk around town (or the city tour) visiting places like the Parliament buildings (if the assembly isn't sitting, anyone can visit), and look into the unusual concrete Holy Family Cathedral along the way (use the map in *What's On* to find your way). Nearby is the cylindrical Kenyatta Conference Center which is used as a conference center for third-world meetings—lovely.

For railroad buffs, there's a historical museum near the railroad station that reflects the city's history from the late 1890's with four trains used along the Mombasa-Lake Victoria line.

If you love beautiful fabrics, perhaps you'd like to see the factory where the famous maridadi fabrics are made. Members of our group were taken there by a friend—very interesting (they bought a lot too). It's out in one of the poorer suburbs, so hire a taxi or a car. Also in this area is the Kamba Carvers Cooperative where good buffalo and antelope figures are made. Just ask where.

The Municipal Market and the Handicraft Centre on Muindi Mbinga Street, opposite the 680 Hotel, I found disappointing, but perhaps you won't.

The University of Nairobi is a lovely and modern place. Well worth a visit.

You can purchase several pounds of Kenya coffee, called black gold by some in several Nairobi shops (there's one down from the Hilton on Mama Ngina Street, near the cinema; these proved to be very welcome gifts). Don't wait to do this at the airport—if you have a late flight, most likely the coffee counter will be closed.

Cross Kenyatta Avenue to Woolworths for any item you may have forgotten—they have everything.

Or set aside some time to learn Swahili. Here are some useful words: *Jambo*—pronounced jahm-bo—is the standard greeting in Kenya for "Hello." *Habari* is "How are you?" and the response is *mzuri,* meaning O.K. or *mzuri sana*—very fine.

HOTELS IN NAIROBI — Accommodations are excellent in this third-world capital—so good that many large organizations hold conventions here hence the need for the spacious Kenyatta Conference Center. So in the deluxe category, there's the New Stanley, a Block hotel, which has been popular with safari groups for years (note: prices keep changing so they will not be quoted, but they are as high, let's say, as a good hotel in Philadelphia). Located downtown on the busy corner of Kenyatta Avenue and Kimathi Street, it's perfect for shopping. But it's not air-conditioned, except for the suites, so if you arrive in the warm winter months be prepared for the heat and the traffic noise through the open windows. A tip: ask for a room on Kimathi or Standard Streets, they are a bit quieter.

Down the street is the cylindrical, and striking Hilton; it's deluxe too, and usually mobbed with tour groups. Its dining facilities are excellent and more extensive than the New Stanley's. The rooms are decorated in an African motif, which put off a friend, but they are air-conditioned.

Another Block hotel, is the venerable Norfolk, a good 5 minute taxi ride from the downtown shopping area. A tip: ask for a room in the new air-conditioned wing. This hotel is a favorite with many as it oozes with colonial charm (perhaps that's why its rates are more expensive than the New Stanley's). The Serena is out from the downtown too in a parklike setting. Another hotel is the downtown Inter-Continental which was building a much needed 200 rocm wing when we were there.

EXTENSIONS FROM NAIROBI — We were going to fly 300 miles to Mombasa on the coast to soak up some sun and rest, but the closing of the border and the resulting airline problems forced us to change our plans. (Note: this mileage was included in the excursion fare rate.) Everyone raves about Mombasa, and it's mobbed, especially in the winter months with Europeans, so it must be worth a visit. I've been told to try the Peponi at Lamu, above Mombasa for a more off-beat flavor, or the Leopard Beach Hotel on the South shore for more modern facilities.

About Lamu: the Peponi Hotel comes highly recommended, meaning the beach, food and service are excellent. Also the town of Lamu has good bargains in wood carvings. Visit the Lamu Museum if you can. A tip: remember any spot on the coast will be more humid, so plan accordingly.

Another spot to consider is the Seychelles—the Islands of Love. I hear the sea shells and bird life are magnificent.

Or try an extension to Tanzania.

One thing I'd like to do is take a walking safari for a few days. To be at eye level with the animals would be exciting.

There are other safaris too—such as the one to Rwanda/Zaire. Or you can make up your own, the cost isn't that much more.

OTHER OPTIONS — Businessmen with a few extra days in Nairobi will find it's easy to obtain tour packages (manytimes these tours are cheaper than the same package booked in the U.S.; some of the Nairobi based tour operators are—Kenya Mystery Tours, African Roadways, Across Africa Safaris, United, and many more). A tip: it's possible to rent-a-car and drive from spot-to-spot too, but remember Kenya's roads aren't interstates. Too, you can camp in the various parks, but you'll have to cope with herds possibly going through your campsite at night.

Reading Suggestions

Your trip can be enriched by reading or rereading one or more of the following books. Take this book along with you as well as those with an asterisk.

Adamson, George. *A Lifetime with Lions.* Garden City: Doubleday, 1968.
Adamson, Joy. *Born Free.* New York: Bantam, 1960.
Adamson, Joy. *Living Free.* New York: Bantam, 1961.
Adamson, Joy. *Forever Free.* New York: Bantam, 1962.
Adamson, Joy. *The Peoples of Kenya.* New York: Harcourt, 1967.
Adamson, Joy. *The Spotted Sphinx.* New York: Harcourt, 1969.
Adamson, Joy. *Pippa's Challenge.* New York: Harcourt, 1972.
Adamson, Joy. *Joy Adamson's Africa.* New York: Harcourt, 1972.
Beard, Peter H. *The End of the Game.* New York: Doubleday, 1963.
Bolles, Edmund Blair. *Fodor's Animal Parks of Africa.* New York: McKay, 1979.
Dominis, John and Edey, Maitland. *The Cats of Africa.* New York: Time, 1968.
Douglas-Hamilton, Iain & Oria. *Among the Elephants.* New York: Viking, 1975.
Dinesen, Isak. *Out of Africa.* New York: Vintage, 1937.
Hulme, Kathryn. *Look a Lion in the Eye.* Boston: Atlantic-Little Brown, 1974.
Jorden, Paul J. *Surgeon on Safari.* New York: Hawthorn, 1976.
Kane, Robert S. *Africa A to Z.* Garden City: Doubleday, 1961.
Leslie-Melville, Betty & Jock. *Elephant Have Right of Way.* Garden City: Doubleday, 1973.
Leslie-Melville, Betty & Jock. *Raising Daisy Rothschild.* New York: Simon and Schuster, 1977.
*Maberly, C.T. Astley. *Animals of East Africa.* London: Hodder & Stoughton, 1960.
Matthiessen, Peter and Porter, Eliot. *The Tree Where Man Was Born. The African Experience.* Dutton: New York, 1972.
Van Lawick-Goodall, Hugo & Jane. *Innocent Killers.* Boston: Houghton Mifflin, 1971.
*Williams, John G. *A Field Guide to the Birds of East and Central Africa.* Boston: Houghton Mifflin, 1963.
Williams, John G. *A Field Guide to the National Parks of East Africa.* Boston: Houghton Mifflin, 1967.

Booklets to purchase in Nairobi:

Kenya: Land of Many Faces. Nairobi: Salama, 1971.
**161 Key Swahili Words and How To Use Them.* Nairobi: Salama, 1971.

Articles from *National Geographic:*

Foster, Bristol. *Africa's Gentle Giants.* Sept. 1977, pp. 402-417.
Gore, Rick and Blair, Jonathan. *A Bad Time to Be a Crocodile.* Jan. 1978, pp. 90-115.
Patterson, Carolyn Bennett. *Rescuing the Rothschild.* Sept. 1977, pp. 419-421.

Other articles:

Grimond, John. *Back to Back. A Survey of Kenya and Tanzania.* The Economist, March 11, 1978, beginning on p. 64.

Index

Acknowledgements

MANY PEOPLE make a book successful. Especially those who go the "extra mile" in support and creative criticism. Ron Smith, the travel editor of the *Philadelphia Inquirer* is a person like this. To him, I'm very grateful for reading the manuscript (and loving it) as well as offering helpful suggestions which made this a better book.

Also, I'm very grateful to H. Ross Watson, the owner of The Photo Center in Bryn Mawr, for his generosity in lending me his 300 mm Nikkor lens to use throughout the safari. Too, it's a blessing to have all my darkroom work done once again by Salvatore De Stefano at the Photo Center; he has made and remade these photographs to fit the size limitations more often than I care to count. In short, he's been wonderful.

There are others too like my typesetter, Mary Ann Ostberg, who labored under a deadline.

And last but not least, I want to acknowledge my wonderful husband, Fred, my companion on all my journeys. Without him, this trip would not have the same meaning.

About the Author

BARBIE ENGSTROM is the creator, author, photographer and publisher of *Engstrom's Travel Experience Guides.* Born in 1937 in Milwaukee, Wisconsin her education includes a B.S. in biology from Northwestern University, a M.S. in endocrinology and biochemistry from New York University and work on a Ph.D. at the University of Pennsylvania Medical School. She has almost taken Dr. Eliot Porter's route to writing and photography in that her career began in the research laboratory, led to medical writing and the establishment of a medical abstracting firm to travel writing and photography all over the world. She has written other guidebooks like *Paris To See and Enjoy,* and she regularly does articles for the travel section of the *Philadelphia Inquirer.* She is also managing director of the non-profit Christian ministry, Kurios Foundation. She and her husband, Fred, who is a fine color photographer and an investment banker, own Kurios Press.

AFRICAN COLOR FOLIO

By Fred Engstrom

East Africa

Listen to the silence of the wind in the grasses:
the high sweep of harrier hawk, quartering the land
in Euclidian flight.

Listen at mid-day to the equatorial sun
casting shadows shapeless as puddles underfoot,
prism-fractured by comet-tailed birds—
turquoise and amethyst, emerald and ruby—igniting
lifeless branches where elephant have passed.

Listen to the peer of cheetah from the latticed greenbush
of a kopje. Listen in the night to the metered wail
of fruit bats, to the stillness following the screaming
of baboons, pursued in their treetops by leopard.

Listen to the silence of the wind in the grasses:
the fugitive flight of antelope before the lion;
the muffled munch of wildebeest—cave bison
endlessly charcoaled against the plain—moving
with giraffe and curious-staring zebra
in a Christmas-ark dream . . . Moving,
all together, back beyond the cratered hills
(like deflated balloons) back past Noah,
back, back to the playtime of Creation.

Listen to the African silence . . .

Listen to the silence of the wind in the grasses.

. . . back past Noah, back, back to the playtime of Creation.

Listen to the silence of the wind in the grasses:

the fugitive flight of antelope before the lion . . .

Listen at mid-day to the equatorial sun . . .

moving with giraffe . . . in a Christmas-ark dream

Listen to the peer of the cheetah from the latticed greenbush.

Listen to the African silence .